LANGUAGE
MAKING
NATURE

A HANDBOOK
FOR WRITERS
ARTISTS AND
THINKERS

DAVID LUKAS

*For Chris,
In memory
of
Yosemite!*

Printed and bound in Dexter, Michigan
by Thomson-Shore, Inc.

ISBN 978-0-9834891-2-2
Library of Congress Control Number: 2015915851

First Printing

Cover photo: Imprint of original trailhead sign on
lichen-covered boulder, Yosemite National Park.
By Jade Wolff.

For Jade

ACKNOWLEDGMENTS

I WOULD LIKE TO THANK Gary Snyder for his long friendship, for challenging me to think deeply about language in all its forms, and for inspiring me to be a writer. Casey Walker introduced me to Keith Basso's work when she asked me to write a review of one of his books in her legendary journal, *Wild Duck Review*, which sparked the ideas that later evolved into this book. James Houlihan did more than he ever imagined when he suggested that I pick up a copy of Calvert Watkins's *How to Kill a Dragon* and then put up with my pestering questions about how to understand this very complex text. I am also grateful that Texas Tech University granted me a Formby Research Fellowship in 2006 so I could study the archived papers of Barry Lopez and devote two months to thinking carefully about language, landscape, and human communities. I am honored that Betsy Livingstone and Susan Traynor read and made valuable comments on an early draft of my manuscript, and I want to express my gratitude for the copyediting work of Jess Beebe at Waxwing Book Studio. As always, it's been a tremendous pleasure to design and produce a book under the expert guidance of David Comstock at Comstock Bonanza Press. Finally, I want to thank Jade Wolff for her love and bright spirit—she has been my beacon and joy from the moment I started hammering out this manuscript on an old typewriter.

CONTENTS

Language
Making
Nature

Rusted, the chain cannot follow.

INTRODUCTION

"Great Britain, whose children we are, and whose language we speak, should no longer be our standard; for the taste of her writers is already corrupted, and her language on the decline."
—Noah Webster, 1789

"The new circumstances under which we are placed, call for new words, new phrases, and the transfer of old words to new objects."
—Thomas Jefferson, August 16, 1813

"Judicious neology can alone give strength and copiousness to language, and enable it to be the vehicle of new ideas."
—Thomas Jefferson, January 27, 1821

I REMEMBER as a child, and as a young budding naturalist, spending all my time observing and testing the world around me—moving pieces, altering the flow of things, and documenting ways the world responded to me. Now, as an adult and a professional naturalist, I've approached language in the same way, not from an academic point of view but as a curious child still building little mud dams in creeks and chasing after frogs. So this book is an odd thing: it is a naturalist's walk through the language-making landscape of the English language, and following in the naturalist's tradition it combines observation, experimentation, speculation, and documentation—activities we don't normally associate with language.

This book is about testing, experimenting, and playing with language. It is a handbook of tools and techniques for taking words apart and putting them back together again in ways that I hope are meaningful and legitimate (or even illegitimate). This book is about peeling back layers in search of the language-making energy of our time. It is about the gaps in meaning that we urgently need to notice and name—the places where our dreams and ideals are no longer fulfilled by a society that has become fast paced and hypercommercialized.

Language is meant to be a playful, ever-shifting creation, but we have been taught—and most of us continue to believe—that language must obediently follow precisely prescribed rules that govern clear sentence structures, specific word orders, correct spellings, and proper pronunciations. If you make a mistake or step out of bounds, there are countless self-appointed language experts who will promptly push you back into safe terrain and scold you for your errors. And in case you need reminding, there are hundreds of dictionaries and grammar books to ensure that you remember the "right" way to use English.

With this backdrop and training in mind, it might come as a bit of a shock to discover that this "ideology of language"—with its preening emphasis on "correctness, authority, prestige, and legitimacy"—represents only one small blip in the long and rich history of the English language. And, for better or worse, we live in a moment in history when a tightly controlled language, economy, and political system work together to create a culture of lies that best serves a powerful elite, allowing them to continue funneling power and money (i.e., influence) to themselves at great cost to human communities and natural ecosystems.

In its heart and soul, language can also be a revolutionary force, and it can be used to expose lies, but you cannot have a revolution if you use the language of the conquerors. So one goal of this book is to awaken language and explore the capacity that all of us possess to be alive in our language. Being awake and being alive is in itself a revolutionary act—something Noah Webster, Thomas Jefferson, and many other important early American thinkers were keenly aware of.

In our busy modern lives we have largely forgotten that language is meant to be inventive and playful, that beneath the veneer of modernity the English language is potent with ancient magic-making power. Throughout this book I will refer repeatedly to "play," but I'm not speaking about play as something trivial; I'm speaking of play as something profoundly creative and freeing. And underneath everything, this playful exploration of language is about dissent, about rising up and crying out in support of that which is alive and vital. This book is about imagination, about truth telling and contemplation; it is an undertaking that is fierce, creative, and honest.

∼ ∼ ∼

MY OWN JOURNEY toward language was sparked in 1996 when I discovered Keith Basso's astonishing book *Wisdom Sits in Places*. Writing about the unique place-making language of the Western Apache, Basso described language in a way that I'd never considered before, as roots and fragments strung together to sing of the land. This idea intrigued me so much that I began carrying Donald Borror's classic little book, *Dictionary of Word Roots and Combining Forms*, with me on all my hikes (a practice I've continued on a daily basis for nearly twenty years and on thousands of miles of trails) in order to learn the meaning and origin of word elements at the moment they occurred to me while walking in wild landscapes.

For many years this seemed little more than a quirky hobby, with no real intent or direction, but then a friend introduced me to Calvert Watkins's magisterial survey of Indo-European poetics, *How to Kill a Dragon*. In a flash I realized that there might be untapped ways for the English language to speak of the magic of the land and the depths of the human spirit, so I began a four-year quest to read every book I could find on the history, formation, and word-making processes of the English language.

What you hold here is the result of my investigation: seventy-six sections that explore some of the many pieces and processes that have gone into shaping the English language as we use it today. As I researched and wrote each section of this book, I carried these ideas with me on long hikes in wild places and held them up against the natural world to see which ideas resonated and which ideas took on a life of their own. This book emerges from and reflects these hikes, and because I also lead walks as a naturalist in my professional life, this book is modeled on the metaphysic that I know best—the flow of ideas and observations that arise spontaneously when humans encounter the world with curiosity and wonder. It feels artificial to offer a table of contents or an index for a journey like this, so this book might seem a little confusing at first, but I trust and hope that this apparent lack of structure invites you to discover something new and unexpected each time you step into the book (just as you would experience on a nature walk).

This book is full of ideas that many people will find strange and complex, so wherever possible I offer examples of each creative process at work. Some of my examples look downright silly, even to me, and I apologize for that. But it's the spirit of the creative process to get the ball rolling by brainstorming and expressing ideas without passing judgment, and I felt that that playful openness and willingness to take chances was more important than self-consciously editing my own examples (as if *I* knew what the ideal models should look like).

Language experts and linguists might take exception to a few of my descriptions and conclusions, and some of their complaints may be valid, but keep in mind that this book is not about technically perfect processes or perfectly formed words; this book is about the wild, creative energy that generates language. Ultimately, this language-making energy is democratic and freely available to all of us no matter what the experts tell you.

At multiple points in this book I invite you to experiment with language and not worry about making mistakes, because culture will always come along to prune your contributions. What I mean by this is that if you make up intriguing new words, and if you use them in the telling of meaningful stories, then your culture *might* adopt your words and mold them into shapes that will endure over time even if your initial contributions seem awkwardly formed or silly looking at first.

If this doesn't make sense, consider a word like *ravisshe*, which Chaucer invented in 1374 in the sense 'to seize' (from the Old French word *ravir*). Chaucer's word almost certainly looked ridiculous and out of place when he first introduced it, but in its subsequently pruned form, *ravish*, it has endured for over 600 years—and that's exactly what might happen to your words, so you can trust this process.

My hope is that this book helps you, or inspires you, to create new words that are sensuous and meaningful in their contours; words that work to express your own deeply felt experiences in the world. The challenge—your challenge—is to open up language and experiment fearlessly, because other people will always come along after you to close language back up again.

This concept of opening up language will be unfamiliar to most people, so it might help to realize that the cycle of opening and closing lies at the very heart of this dynamic, flexible language we call English. Over and over again, revolutions and seismic shifts have come along to break down rigid conventions and open up language; then prescriptivists have stepped in with rules that reestablish order and close things back up again. Think of Chaucer, who is said to have added 1100 new words to the English language while "inventing" English poetry; consider Shakespeare and his astoundingly influential body of work; or look at Lewis and Clark, who added 1500 words to the English language while attempting to describe a continent that no European had written about before.

Each of these writers, and many others beside them, came along at a moment when nothing was cut and dry, when nothing was worn out. These are the moments when language sparkles, when it has the freedom to express new values and new ideals. But these moments of freedom are also deeply unsettling for many people, so things eventually get closed up again, and anyone who steps out of line will be corrected and edited—both literally and figuratively.

I look around at my culture, at the ways that people treat each other and at the ways that people treat the land, and I feel that we live in one of those times when language is closed and guarded by gatekeepers. I read Thoreau's *Walden* and realize that the language we use to speak of the natural world, and of our relationship with the natural world, has changed very little in 150 years. And if the language we use to speak of the natural world is not innovative and engaging, then is it any wonder that few young people get excited about nature?

I feel that the time has come for language to shine again, to bloom like a flower and lead the way as we begin to speak confidently about the future we want. But this can only happen when we create new words that will serve as vessels for new ideas and new dreams. Long-stable systems and stale old conventions are already breaking down before our eyes, and in the midst of this teetering balance we have an amazing opportunity to rebuild our culture and our relationship with the natural world through language.

It's clear that experimenting with and reshaping an entire language would lead to chaos, and that's not the intent of this book, but it would be okay if we started by experimenting with one field of language. I propose that our language of nature is the perfect place to begin. It's the one domain where language should be wild and trailless and prickly anyway, so why can't it lead the way?

But isn't it a mistake to make words harder to understand and use? Don't we want to make it easier to read about the natural world so that people feel welcome, rather than making the path more complicated? Paradoxically, scientists have discovered that people are much better learners when words are hard to understand, because it creates what psychologists call *desirable difficulties*. In fact, our brains are wired to grapple with difficulties, and it turns out that we almost instantly forget or dismiss things that are easily understood. Studies have found, for instance, that students remember more and have better learning comprehension when they are given materials that are written in ugly or difficult-to-read lettering, because these desirable difficulties lead to *productive frustration*. Frustration sounds like a bad thing, but it slows us down, increases our engagement, awakens our curiosity, and creates mysteries that our brains love to solve. Doesn't it make sense then that strange, oddly formed, or broken words—all described in this book—would have the same effect?

From my study of the long trajectory of the English language, I believe that it is absolutely vital that we keep shapeshifting our words. Once locked in place, everything contained within the vessel of a word (its spelling, meaning, connotation, sound, etc.) becomes mundane and familiar. A word soon loses its magic-making power, as well as its connection to something vibrant and alive "out there" in the world—and this process can only diminish our deep bond with the natural world as it speaks to us through words. It is essential for our survival that we continue to create innovative new words that require and reward our attention, and that we engage in this process so we stay awake and alive.

Purists will argue that new words still need to follow well-established rules. And yes, it's true that you can study and familiarize yourself with these rules, but in all human endeavors there are people who follow rules and those who ignore or break them. Someone who follows the rules contributes rigor and consistency, but the rule breaker is more likely to make unexpected contributions and leaps of the imagination. It will be up to you which path you want to take, and neither choice is right or wrong.

Either way, the intent of this language-making task should always be toward the refinement of language for the sake of an entire community, rather than on an individual showing off and confusing readers with odd or overly elaborated words. Strive for simplicity, clarity, and beauty in the sound and shape of each word you create, and remember that little of this book will be meaningful unless these language-making processes and new words are used in the telling of great stories.

This is the task of our time.

"To make a revolution every day is the nature of the sun."

—Sir Thomas Browne, 1642

VOICES AND GODS

IMAGINE YOU are casually walking in the woods one day and you suddenly become conscious of your thoughts. What is the first thing you notice? Most likely, you become aware of "voices" in your head.

To the ancient Greeks these voices were the voices of the gods speaking to humans, and to preliterate cultures for which we have no records these could have been the voices of nature itself.

So, what if those voices were the spirits of the natural world speaking to you, instead of (or in addition to) being your own private thoughts? What would it be like to begin naming the voices you hear in your head and begin giving them the personalities of plants, animals, and places that are welcoming and including you in their world?

If this sounds a bit crazy, keep in mind that this kind of awareness was a vital component of ancient Greek literature, poetry, and mythology, which is the foundation of our modern culture. Maybe it's not so crazy after all; maybe it's one way that culture can be created.

❧

Laurens Van der Post writing about Bushmen of the Kalahari:
"wherever they went, they felt they were known"

❧

THREE-DIMENSIONAL WORDS

I BEGAN THINKING about the dimensionality of words after reading a haunting passage in David Abram's book *Becoming Animal*, in which he describes watching Tibetan monks stamping carved wood-block prayers onto the surface of a flowing river so that the ephemeral imprints of their prayers could be carried to the ocean. This image has continued to resonate for me: the idea that flowing water could activate and lift the meaning of words from their printed representations as readily as the human mind "lifts" words from the page when we read a book.

We usually think of words as flat and passive two-dimensional symbols on a printed page, while missing the fact that printed words are a relatively modern development that radically alters our sense of what is real and important. Abram rightly cautions that we have become so accustomed to staring at flat representations (billboards, televisions, computer screens, printed pages) that we have become thoroughly trained to look *at* the surface of, rather than *into* the depths of, the living world around us.

There is a legendary story about the famous Harvard zoologist Louis Agassiz asking a prospective student to describe a fish. Agassiz placed the dead fish in front of the student and left the room with the command that the student should jot down everything he could about the fish. After ten minutes the student had a list of features that described the fish, perhaps something along the lines of "it's a scaly, laterally compressed, aquatic animal." But the professor was nowhere to be found, so the bored student was forced to sit with the fish for several more hours until Agassiz finally returned and asked the student what he had observed. The student reported what he had learned about the fish, but Agassiz told him his observations were not good enough and that the student needed to look at the fish again. After three exhausting days of staring at the fish, Agassiz was finally satisfied that the student had learned how to see the "fish" within the fish, then promptly gave the student a new fish to observe, and then another, and another, for eight months straight.

Abram offers another telling example of our tendency to focus on the flat representation of a thing while entirely missing its depth. He points out that we think of shadows as flattened outlines on the ground while overlooking the obvious truth that shadows occupy three-dimensional space. In fact, all you have to do is extend your hand into a projected shadow to verify that it occupies space and that the outline on the ground is merely the barest portion of the shadow's entire volume.

So too with words. In the same way we see only a shadow's outline, or neglect to investigate "fishness," we overlook or miss the depth of words. No word is passive; every single word has an influence on us, and this influence extends far beyond the mere outline of a shape on a flat page.

What would happen, for instance, if we traced with our fingers a single word in the snow or in the mud, or wrote a word on a leaf, and then returned hour after hour, day after day, to witness the word over time. Not that there is any special significance in the decaying word itself, but the devoted apprenticeship to the word might open up space for a shift from "looking at" to "looking into." And once learned with one word, these observation skills could be practiced with another word and then another word.

There are so many ways to think about the depth, or dimensionality, of words that an entire book could be written on the subject. There are dimensions such as time and emotional content and meaning and history, not to mention the physical lifting of the word into the world as practiced by Tibetan monks. Early Greeks had the magical idea that every word had a unique existence and essence each time it was used. Language was a living force for these ancient peoples because they had an active and dynamic relationship with each word every time they used it. This is the kind of intimacy we might rediscover by reaching once again into the shadows to investigate the depth and dimensionality of words.

Words are not merely flat objects on a page but multidimensional objects that are malleable and "out there" in space; we can hold words in our hands or in our minds as we shape, view, and experience them. The oral tradition seems to come closest to this idea, but with practice maybe we could preserve this awareness even with words on a printed page. All we need to do is to keep shaping words with the consciousness that they have depth and layers of meaning beyond their superficial outlines.

୧ଛ

"Words that lean on the mind are no good. They must dent it."
—Whitaker and Baker
(America's first political
consultants)

୧ଛ

CROSSING BOUNDARIES

What if

HUMANS LOVE TO put boundaries around things because boundaries help us make sense of our lives. But boundaries have a way of becoming hard edges, and over time they make us lose sight of the fact that all things are porous and interconnected. For instance, the word *lake* might be a convenient label when you point to the middle of a large body of water, but how do you define a lake's boundaries where its waves lap ephemerally against the shoreline, or when its shoreline is a marsh, or when the streams flowing into or out of the lake belong to the same body of water? As soon as you try to map precise boundaries in the real world, you discover that an idealized thing like a lake has no easily defined edges.

the boundaries

Boundaries are lines we think exist but that dissolve upon inspection, and this realization leads to some important questions: How and why do we make boundaries? And what happens if we venture beyond the boundaries we draw around things?

of your kingdom

These questions are equally relevant in languages because there is more fuzziness than we like to admit in the lines we draw around words and meanings. The word *lake*, for example, has had many different shapes in English, including *lac, laca, lace, lack, lacke, lacku, lacu, laik*, and *leke*, yet modern English speakers hold onto *lake* as if this single spelling had a fence around it. And if you try to apply meaning to the word *lake*, how small can you go before you are talking about a pond, or how fast can the water flow before it is a river?

were ethical

In terms of language this raises vital questions, such as how many letters can be changed before a word is no longer the same word, or how far can you stretch a definition without losing its meaning. Is there a limit to how far you can take these changes, and what happens as you approach or cross over that line?

rather than physical?

The liminal space where you cross out of the known and into the unknown is where language opens up. Consider, for example, that uncertain edge where a meadow blends into a forest. What happens in the real world, in your definitions of words, and in the linguistic forms you use as you cross from this thing called a "meadow" into this thing called a "forest"? Is there a point where a meadow is no longer a meadow but is not yet a forest, and how do you define those spaces where there are no convenient pegs to hang words and meanings on? If your society tries to convince you that things and words and meanings such as *lake* or *meadow* or *forest* are clearly bounded, then maybe it is time to start investigating those boundaries, because on the other side there are going to be new words, new spellings, and new meanings.

ﷺ

The mountains take their pencil to my spirit as I sleep,
sketching in lines of memory and long canyons
waiting to draw me in upon rising.

ﷺ

BOUNDARIES OF WORDS

o ur liqui dgods pourfrom themoun tains
rockun der cliff
lando' t'lin ede arth
butI bearyou hunt
oo-owl

ALTHOUGH WE HAVE become accustomed to and attached
to the expectation that each word has a specific shape and
spelling (especially with modern dictionaries and mass media
repeatedly emphasizing the "correct" forms), it is important to
remember that there are no sacred or god-given reasons why
words must have certain spellings or word boundaries. It has
been noted, for instance, that Shakespeare spelled his own
name in a different way each time he wrote it.

In his book *A Guide to Chaucer's English*, David Burnley
notes that different forms of words comfortably existed side
by side with each other in Middle English. He gives examples
of *thin aunt* alongside *thy naunt*, *the othir* alongside *tothir*, and
at the fulle alongside *ate fulle*. It is notable that not only the
spelling of these words shifts but also the sense of where the
boundary of each word begins and ends.

The idea that words must have specific and known boundaries (what psychologists call *Bouma shapes*), as well as firmly
established spellings, is a relatively recent development that
helped signal the transition from Middle English into Early
Modern English. However, this idea is nothing more than a
mutually understood compact—it is not a universal law or a
higher authority.

Language immediately becomes a more vivid and creative

tool if you keep Middle English examples in mind and let go of modern conventions. The boundaries of individual words can be shifted, expanded, contracted, or dropped altogether; these choices can even be varied between uses. The way that a text is read aloud does not need to change (although shifts in boundaries might lead to novel pronunciations); what matters is that boundary shifts profoundly alter the ways that readers perceive and engage with texts.

§⋅

"All intellectual substance which has been given form can in turn become the material of new creations."
—Ernst Robert Curtius,
*European Literature and
the Latin Middle Ages*

§⋅

AN OUTLINE OF ENGLISH WORD FORMATION

THE IDEA OF forming new words, and having permission to form new words, is a novelty for most people, so it might help to realize that word formation is a legitimate activity of considerable interest to scholars of language. In fact, for the English language there is a significant body of literature on this topic, inspired in part by Hans Marchand's seminal book *The Categories and Types of Present-Day English Word-Formation*.

Linguists quibble over details but essentially recognize

three primary processes of word formation in English—affixation, compounding, and conversion—with the rest of our new words arising from three other, more or less informal, processes—blending, clipping, and word manufacturing. An understanding of these processes can help guide you in thinking about new words, but these processes do not need to be memorized or thought of as limitations, because word formation is first and foremost an act of creativity.

Affixation

The most common and basic way to form new words is to add affixes (prefixes or suffixes) to root words. This is a straightforward process because most affixes are familiar and easily recognized, and because the concept of affixation is taught to students at an early age. Thus, we can easily point to simple word constructions like *pre+fix, sub+conscious, short+en*, or *green+ish*, as well as to more complex constructions such as *ad+mir+a+ble*. Many affixes have a long history of use, with their original forms and meanings either preserved over time or else modified in various ways (e.g., the Latin suffix *-ibilis* is now spelled *-able* or *-ible*). Affixes are usually thought of as fragments that depend on other words, but many started out as independent words that became dependent through repeated combination with other words.

Creating your own words with affixes could happen in several different ways. You could start with any of the conventional, familiar affixes and simply use them in new combinations. For example, you could come up with a word like *antiforest* to mean 'a clearcut,' or you could create an adjective from the mythological Medusa by adding *-ant* to form the word *medusant*. I have had a lot of fun tracking down obscure words and roots and giving them new life by adding affixes; for instance, taking the scientific name for otters, *Lutra*, and turning it into *lutrine* to speak of the sinuous flow of a river, or taking the root *argent*, meaning 'silver,' and turning it into *argentine* to describe silvery mountain peaks (interestingly, I later found both of these examples in *The Oxford English Dictionary*, which I took as confirmation that this is a valid word-forming process).

In addition to familiar affixes, there are large numbers of archaic, forgotten, or rarely used affixes that could be made productive again. While it is possible that these neglected affixes were left behind for good reasons—they might form awkward-sounding words, or they might have been replaced by more useful affixes—it is also possible they were left behind simply because they fell out of favor and were forgotten, or because the sounds they created were not fashionable in a given era. This could include affixes from other languages that were rejected because they looked strange when they were first tried. However, the novelty and lovely sounds of unfamiliar affixes can be part of their charm and can lead to their widespread acceptance no matter how old or foreign the source.

Some of the best places to look for old affixes might be in Latin, Anglo-Saxon, and Old French dictionaries, not because these languages are somehow more valid but because so many of our modern affixes already come from these sources and there is great value in keeping a language coherent by drawing from analogous sources. A long-unused Latin affix, for example, would be meaningful because it is "part of the family" and has some type of kinship with the rest of our modern vocabulary. Likewise, affixes might be drawn from other historically significant languages such as Old Norse, Old Germanic, Spanish, or Italian, all of which have contributed to the historic formation of English.

It is also legitimate, and potentially highly productive, to give both old and modern affixes new forms by dropping, adding, or changing some of their letters. This has already happened countless times in the creation of our modern affixes (sometimes in unexpected ways, as with the radical transformation of the Latin suffix *-ium* into English *-e*, which turned *silentium* into *silence*). This process would be particularly useful if you were bringing forward archaic affixes that look unwieldy to the modern eye (for example, old Anglo-Saxon affixes like *-feald*, *-raeden*, or *-scipe* might prove useful if given new forms).

Compounding

One simple, and very prolific, way of making new words is to combine two words or roots to suggest an alternate meaning. The resulting compound may be hyphenated (*fast-food*), merged (*anyone*), or written as two words (*bulletin board*). A compound can be a more specific type of its components (a *nosebleed* may be a type of nose that is bleeding or a type of bleeding in the nose), or it may not be a type of its components at all (a *skinhead* is not a type of skin nor a type of head).

Almost any combination of form classes (nouns, verbs, adjectives, etc.) can be put together (see *English Word-Formation* by Laurie Bauer, and *An Introduction to Modern English Word-Formation* by Valerie Adams, for discussions of the possible combinations), but noun+noun combinations are by far the most productive in English. In addition, it helps to be aware of some minor or traditional modifications that facilitate awkward letter combinations in newly joined compounds. For instance, an *i* is often inserted in words compounded from Latin sources (e.g., *ped-i-cure*), while an *o* is added in Greek compounds (e.g., *micr-o-scope*).

Compounds are not only ubiquitous in English but also phenomenally productive in helping describe the natural world because they can make unfamiliar, nonhuman objects more familiar or comforting by naming them in ways that resonate with the human imagination. Compounds can be especially playful and creative because they are free to link wildly different elements such as descriptive terms, anthropocentric references, mythological themes, and mundane objects in unexpected ways. Consequently, the range of compound words used to describe the natural world is not only astonishing but also revealing and inspiring; just look at how versatile compounding is in the formation of nature words such as *rattlesnake, dragonfly, seahorse, bullfrog, tapeworm, storksbill, goldfield, sunflower, bluebells, blackbird, hummingbird, mockingbird, driftwood, earthbound, moth-eaten, stone-cold, sun-baked, waterlogged, honeycomb, pigeonhole, spread-eagle, leapfrog, horseback, henpeck, rainbow, waterfall, downhill, downstream, underbrush, overseas,* and *outdoors.* A skilled writer could create an entirely new vocabulary of nature words through compounding alone.

Conversion

Conversion is an easily overlooked process of word formation because there is no change in the spelling or sound of a word; a word is simply used as a new part of speech. Though subtle, conversion has been an important and productive mechanism in the development of English. For instance, the noun *table* ("to sit at a table") has been converted into the verb *table* ("to table an issue"). Virtually any element of English can undergo conversion; even an acronym can be converted into a new part of speech. However, most conversions create either nouns or verbs as final products. The only limitation seems to be that a word will not be converted into a new part of speech if that new meaning is already occupied (blocked) by a pre-existing word. Therefore, the noun *arrival* will not be converted into a verb *arrival* if it has the same meaning as the verb *arrive* (a word that already fills the role that a verb *arrival* would take).

Conversion has a tremendous, and largely untapped, potential for speaking of the natural world. I can think of only a few contemporary examples, such as the noun *bloom* (a flower), which was apparently converted into the verb *bloom* in Middle English, or the noun *wolf*, which is thought to have started as an adjective that meant 'dangerous,' then later converted into a noun for a dangerous animal. But why not try out novel conversions like turning the noun *dragonfly* into a verb *dragonfly* ("let's dragonfly around")? Because this sounds so odd at first, it's a good example of how the process works and how playful it can be.

Blending

When parts of words are run together to form new words, the process is called *blending*. In its most abbreviated form, when only the first letter of each word is used, blending creates acronyms (e.g., NATO, YMCA), but blending usually includes more letters from the original words, as in a classic example like *brunch* (breakfast+lunch).

There seem to be very few blended words in nature writing (an exception might be *smog*, from smoke+fog), and I do not know of any writers who have explored this process further, but it has potential. For example, as a naturalist I frequently talk with people who do not see the difference between frogs and toads (*froads?*), or lizards and salamanders (*lizanders?*). These somewhat frivolous blends might be better suited to a Lewis Carroll story, but there is no reason a writer could not use blending in the course of describing a profound, personal experience in nature. The frivolous air of blended words might even be used advantageously to soften the telling of a truly dark and terrifying encounter with the unknown.

Clipping

Clipping is another word-forming process that appears to be vastly underutilized in speaking of the natural world, though it too has potential. Clipping occurs when parts of words come to stand for whole words or phrases, such as when naturalists talk about using *binocs* instead of *binoculars*. Modern society is full of clipped words, especially within groups of people where shared membership fosters the use of colloquial, slang-like code words (groups ranging from hip-hop artists to scientists to construction crews).

People who share a passion for the natural world are one such group, yet their experimentation with clipped words seems rather limited and is not terribly creative (birdwatchers, for example, sometimes refer to Red-tailed Hawks as *red-tails*). Stretching these boundaries might be the work of a writer with a keenly tuned ear for language. For instance, *synth* could be a clipped version of *photosynthesis*, or *decomp* for *decomposition*, or *lopack* for *solo backpacking*.

Word Manufacturing

The invention of words out of thin air, with little connection to the history of a language, is a rare process. In modern society it is mainly used in the formation of brand names for new products, but a few serious writers have dabbled in word manufacturing as well (e.g., Kurt Vonnegut, James Joyce). It is hard to pull this off convincingly, but someone writing about the natural world could conceivably come up with a few useful words this way. The poet Ezra Pound, for instance, manufactured some lovely "nature" words including *Ileuthyeria*, *periplum*, *pitkin*, and *tenthril*. One potential disadvantage of manufactured words, no matter how beautiful, is that they lack depth and history, so they are more like isolated nuggets than rich geologic veins.

Steps in the Creation and Acceptance of New Words

Not all words that are borrowed or created will be accepted by a larger culture, and the process can take hundreds of years. Here is a general outline of the steps by which words seem to work their way into a language (based on T. E. Hope, *Lexical Borrowing in the Romance Languages*).

- Once a word is introduced, it goes through an initial stage of fluctuation and experimentation in which different forms or uses of the word are tested.

- This leads to temporary success or rejection as the word is measured against the formal conventions of the language it is being introduced to.

- There might then be further shifts as the word is molded to fit the structure of the receiving language.

- This leads to increasing stabilization and crystallization as the word enters common usage, often through the influence of a prominent text or individual.

- The final form of the word is then "authenticated" and protected from further modifications.

One thing to notice about these steps is that cultures have a rather complex and drawn out process for "vetting" new words. And the final products may not preserve the original words that begin this process. What this means for the language-making student is that you do not have to worry about creating perfectly formed words because if necessary your culture will prune each word into the shape it needs or wants.

While this basic outline of English word formation high-lights the amazing potential of the English language to create new words, do not lose sight of the most powerful language-making tool of all: the act of simply pulling forward beautiful old words that have been left behind. Dictionaries of Anglo-Norman, Medieval Latin, and Middle English, not to mention *The Oxford English Dictionary*, spill over with forgotten words so gorgeous they seem magical. Bring these forward and your world will come alive.

*Give us the raw language of what it means to have and to seek a relationship with nature and landscape **in our time**.*

Bring language to life, as in "carrying it with you" into life.

WISDOM SITS IN PLACES

THE BOOK THAT FIRST opened my eyes to the ways that language and the natural world could influence each other was Keith Basso's award-winning *Wisdom Sits in Places*, a book that explores "landscape and language among the Western Apache."

As described by Basso, the Western Apache of east-central Arizona, like indigenous peoples all over the world, pay close attention to the land because it sustains their culture and sense of self. The Western Apache encode their knowledge and engagement with their landscape in elaborate and highly imaginative place-names that not only preserve the memory of their ancestors and the essential moral lessons of their culture but also keep the ancestors and moral lessons alive in an active present tense.

To an outsider these place-names appear to be little more than complex strings of letters, but for the Western Apache the names make pictures of physical locations that they carry in their minds throughout their entire lives, serving as constant reminders of the places and social codes that sustain them as a people. For it is in each of these places that wisdom sits, held as if in watertight vessels, preserved through stories and place-names, readily available whenever a tribal member gets "thirsty" or "runs dry."

This is a profoundly important idea because modern society is losing its places and place-meanings on a daily basis, community by community, and we have few ways of holding or defending these values except through litigation and confrontation. Ultimately, many people engage in the democratic process in order to defend the places they love, and when places are lost it only adds to the apathy we feel about the process. How can we exercise our rights as citizens when we no longer belong to places or have places where we give meaning?

Sadly, the practice of place-naming has been largely lost in modern society, even as the practice is widely abused and mocked by developers, who love to come up with names like "Shady Oak Estates" or "Meadowbrook Farm" after they have plowed some piece of native habitat into oblivion. Developers clearly understand the potent role of place-naming as a mechanism for assigning meaning and controlling dialogue, so why isn't this power utilized by the rest of us? What would it look like if we created our own place-names and filled the land with stories again?

In answer to these questions, it is helpful to look more closely at place-names used by the Western Apache as a model, while keeping in mind that place-names and stories are inseparable; we cannot have one without the other, and when we separate them we end up with places like "Shady Oak Estates."

Even when translated into English, the place-names of the Western Apache have lovely sounds—"Circular Clearing with Slender Cottonwood Trees," "Whiteness Spreads Out Descending to Water," "Line of Blue Below Rocks"—but in their native tongue these place-names are constructed in a symbolic language that native speakers find so beautiful they chant the names tirelessly under their breath like favorite songs.

These place-names are built from long strings of prefixes added to core root verbs, creating highly condensed and highly expressive "sentences" that function as names. When I first read about Western Apache place-names and studied their linguistic structures I thought it was a shame that English could not form place-names in the same way. English simply lacks the ability to form sentence-like strings of unique prefixes. Therefore, Western Apache place-names in the model of *T'iis Ts'ósé Bił Naagolgaiyé* would look like a bunch of unintelligible letters if we tried to do the same thing in English.

However, as a first stab it might work to construct place-names from ordinary English words, creating names like "Sees Canyons and Rivers," "Hollow Holding Place," "Stands Alone in Water," or "Oh Exclamation Ridge." If nothing else, these could be meaningful and potentially evocative ways of naming the landscape and suggesting underlying stories.

But place-names are powerful because they are meant to be meaningful only within specific narratives or for particular communities, rather than needing to enter common usage, which means they do not have to follow typical rules of language and have the potential to be one of the few places where our language can be totally playful and free-form. It seems a shame to limit ourselves to ordinary words when place-names give us a rare opportunity to explore language in a rule-free environment.

Upon further reflection, I eventually realized that English does in fact have its own immense body of words roots and stems that could function as unique place-name elements. Drawing from my favorite sourcebook (Donald Borror's *Dictionary of Word Roots and Combining Forms*), I discovered that it would be possible to use roots and stems to construct intriguing place-names like "Loc-alta-lith" ('Place of High Rocks'; *loc* is the stem for words like location, *alta* means 'high,' and *lith* is an element meaning 'rock') or "Cyano-nama-nao" ('Blue Stream Temple').

In keeping with the idea that place-names are not part of ordinary language and do not need to follow typical language rules, there would be no "right" way to spell these names and you could experiment with unique markers and punctuation. "Loc-alta-lith," for instance, could be written *Loc:alta:lith* or *Loc'altalith*, or any of many other ways. (Note that place-names do not necessarily have to be pronounceable, though they would be most useful if they were constructed so they were beautiful when spoken.) I prefer to use hyphens, because they separate phrase elements and make them easier to understand, but with growing familiarity the hyphens might be dropped in some place-names.

The Western Apache add one other critical element: distinctive enclitics that occur only at the end of place-names to signal that the phrase describes a place and not an object. Elements like *y* or *d* as we use them when we say *y'all* or *we'd* are enclitics. They do not stand alone as words but have some of the features of words and affixes. English has no place-name enclitics, but there is no reason that someone could not come up with some. For example, *'om* (from *home*) could be a place-name marker giving us forms like "Loc'altalith'om."

Basso writes that place-names may also look forward to ask the question, What will happen here? This is an evocative question, but the land holds our stories and we are losing the land so the better question might be, What will happen here if we don't start naming the places we care about?

Our generation is only marginally connected to nature (compared to our parents), but the next generation will have almost no memory of that connection unless we find ways to record it.
(Latin *recorder* 'to pass through the heart again')

"Species of humanity have given way to a universal crowd of individuals whose most salient characteristic is their being identically entertained."
—Jonathan Franzen

PATTERNS IN NATURE

ONE SOURCE OF INSPIRATION for new words could come from observing patterns in nature. The patterns you find may offer new words or beg new words, but either way they are a highly formative aspect of the world around us. Nature presents an unlimited variety of patterns that have never been named—and they are a lot of fun to look for.

Patterns are any kind of design or form notable enough to be considered a model. They may occur as loosely organized, singular moments in time that can be given simple names, or they may occur in tightly structured repeating motifs that suggest a type of poetic meter or rhetoric. Patterns often involve shapes or forms, but they can also arise from any interplay of textures, motions, directions, functions, or units of time. The four seasons, for example, might be a pattern in time, while the organization of a flock of birds sitting on the water compared to a flock of birds flying in the air might be a pattern of function or lifestyle.

All of these structured moments of experience are constantly unfolding around us, but we notice them only when we pay attention. Thus, the act of observing and naming patterns is an act of paying attention, a way in which language helps us stay fully alive to this world of stippling trees, insinuous waves, and eyeline ridges.

❧

Not hammer-strokes, but dance of water sings pebbles into perfection.
—slightly modified from Rabindranath Tagore's poem "Stray Birds"

Put natural history in the heart of a healthy human culture.

❧

SHALLOW NAMES

WHEN WE LOOK out at the natural world around us it might feel like everything is known, or at the very least that everything is named. And while it is true that all known organisms are named, even down to the most obscure mushrooms and microscopic worms, how many of us look closely at these names?

Nearly all the labels for tens of thousands of plants and animals in North America have been given to us by scientists. This lends the names an air of authority and legitimacy, but the surprising fact is that much of this terminology is poverty-stricken: these names are mere place-holders, shallow names with shallow stories behind them.

I say this because the vast majority of these names were concocted by scientists who had little to no experience with an organism's life or character when they named it (species are typically named first and then studied in detail only if someone later takes a special interest in that new species). In the case of North American birds, for example, this has led to anomalous names like Hermit Warbler and Solitary Vireo (birds that were named before their social tendencies had been studied).

An astounding number of names have been created by scientists in museums who have never seen the organisms in their living forms or in their native habitats. There is a sizable degree of arrogance encoded in these names, and they often leave real-world observers scratching their heads. Names like Ring-necked Duck, Sharp-shinned Hawk, Hairy Woodpecker, Northern Beardless-Tyrannulet, and Northern Rough-winged Swallow describe features that might be visible on dead museum specimens but are obscured in real life.

Many other names merely denote superficial features such as colors or shapes, or the geographic locations where organisms were first collected. At an even greater remove are the huge numbers of names that commemorate the male-based system of scientific reciprocity, men naming species after other men as a way of legitimizing each other's "greatness." The list of North American bird names bearing men's surnames is daunting: Cassin's, Cooper's, Hammond's, Harris's, Heermann's, Swainson's, Townsend's, Wilson's, and so on. It is telling that out of some nine hundred North American birds, only three are named after women, and all by their first names only (which was never done for men): Anna's Hummingbird, Grace's Warbler, and Lucy's Warbler.

And sadly, at least in the case of birds, there are very few names that signify spiritual, mythological, or poetic properties. The closest I can find are goatsuckers and ibis, although there is a kind of poetry in names like starling ('little star') or crane ('to cry out').

So does it matter if these names are shallow, and should anything be done about this? There are no easy answers, but it will be difficult for any of us to rethink the natural world when the entire system of knowledge is bounded by a coded language controlled by a single committee of scientists. (All naming rules and choices are decided by the International Commission of Zoological Nomenclature, a group of twenty-eight scientists, only four of whom are women as of this writing.)

When all is said and done, these "technical" names are at best placeholders, rapidly created according to preconceived rules in order to keep pace with the furious rate of discovery (15,000 new species are named each year). The proper role of a scientist, after all, is to discover natural "facts" and keep moving with the frontier of discovery, not to double back and fill in human meaning. So here we are, looking at a world of placeholders, and the question is whether anyone wants to double back and fill in the places these names are holding.

❧

If there are people who promote lies and half-truths, then let them while the rest of us have fun and create energy by speaking of the things we enjoy and find meaningful.

Taken together, this day added to the last and grafted onto the next forms a body of attention, an attentive life which is

not accidental but intentional. I did not need this day to be
unique, but it could have been. I did not need to come home
with a story or a poem, but it would have been fine if I had.
This small piece was instead that measured opening of life,
one beautiful and simple addition to that larger whole
I pay attention to.

THE BLOSSOMING OF LANGUAGE

- *Borrow foreign words!*
- *Coin new words!*
- *Expand the meaning of existing words!*

"And it ought to be remembered that there is nothing
more difficult to take in hand, more perilous to conduct,
or more uncertain in its success, than to take the lead
in the introduction of a new order of things."
—Machiavelli, *The Prince*

Hope shouldn't be a projection outward, but a filling inward
akin to faith or belief
with an added layer of warmth as if standing
face to sun with eyes closed.

BIBLIOGRAPHY

MANY BOOKS HAVE INFLUENCED and informed my thinking about language-making processes in English, some from a technical and some from a reflective point of view, but rather than try to list all of them I have selected a "bookshelf" of titles that have been most influential for me. The dictionaries alone would take up several bookshelves, but some of the ones listed here can be accessed digitally.

General Titles

Abram, David. 2010. *Becoming Animal: An Earthly Cosmology*. New York: Pantheon.

> David Abram's far-ranging explorations of language and sensory experience are astonishingly insightful, and David has taught me how to see the natural world in many new ways.

Basso, Keith. 1996. *Wisdom Sits in Places: Landscape and Language Among the Western Apache*. Albuquerque: University of New Mexico Press.

> I count the moment I read Basso's book in 1996 as the beginning of my journey into language-making, because it opened my eyes to the ways that language (and word roots) could describe the natural world.

Bringhurst, Robert. 2008. *The Tree of Meaning: Language, Mind, and Ecology*. Berkeley: Counterpoint.

> Bringhurst is one of our generation's most important thinkers, and his essays on ecological linguistics and other topics are fascinating.

Watkins, Calvert. 1995. *How to Kill a Dragon: Aspects of Indo-European Poetics*. New York: Oxford University Press.

There are no words to express how profoundly this book has influenced my life. And even though this book is so scholarly that I understand but a fraction of it, I have used and annotated my copy so heavily that it is falling apart. It has been my sourcebook and guiding light through every stage of my thinking. Each time I dip into Watkins's book I catch a few more glimpses into how deeply language and ritual language express the human experience.

Books for Understanding English

Adams, Valerie. 1973. *An Introduction to Modern English Word-Formation*. London: Longman.

This book is useful for taking a different approach to the topic than the textbooks by Bauer, Marchand, and Plag.

Bauer, Laurie. 1983. *English Word-Formation*. Cambridge: Cambridge University Press.

A bit dry and stodgy, but an essential overview of the topic.

Crystal, David. 1995. *The Cambridge Encyclopedia of the English Language*. Cambridge: Cambridge University Press.

An appealing and comprehensive survey of the history and structure of English, with many photographs, graphs, and charts.

Denning, Keith, et al. 2007. *English Vocabulary Elements*. Oxford: Oxford University Press.

This book is a fantastic resource for analyzing and understanding the Greek and Latin elements found in English words.

Durkin, Philip. 2014. *Borrowed Words: A History of Loanwords in English*. Oxford: Oxford University Press.

An interesting book by the deputy chief editor of *The Oxford English Dictionary*.

Emerson, Oliver Farrar. 1894. *The History of the English Language*. New York: Macmillan.

An old and quaint book that is valuable for including insights into the English language that seem to have been left out of modern books.

Hughes, Geoffrey. 2000. *A History of English Words*. Oxford: Blackwell.

An important analysis of the social environments that English evolved in.

Jespersen, Otto. 1909–1949. *A Modern English Grammar on Historical Principles*. Copenhagen.

This seven-volume set is an essential sourcebook on all the sounds, spellings, and syntax structures found in the English language, but these books are so dense and comprehensive that they require close study.

Marchand, Hans. 1969. *The Categories and Types of Present-Day English Word-Formation*. Munich: Beck.

The modern study of English word-formation started with Marchand's seminal book, which remains a definitive compilation of the pieces and processes that go into shaping English words.

Miller, D. Gary. 2006. *Latin Suffixal Derivatives in English and Their Indo-European Ancestry*. Oxford: Oxford University Press.

This book is technical, but once you start digging into it you will be astonished at the many ways that Latin suffixes have deeply transformed the meaning and use of English words. I must be a language nerd, because I have often thought that if I was marooned on an island, this would be one of the half dozen books I'd want to have with me.

Miller, D. Gary. 2012. *External Influences on English:*

From Its Beginnings to the Renaissance. Oxford: Oxford University Press.

> My favorite book for understanding how English has been influenced and shaped by other languages.

Minkova, Donka and Robert Stockwell. 2009. *English Words: History and Structure.* Cambridge: Cambridge University Press.

> A concise and useful summary of the topic.

Plag, Ingo. 2003. *Word-Formation in English.* Cambridge: Cambridge University Press.

> One of the best guides for understanding English word-formation.

Pyles, Thomas. 1964. *The Origins and Development of the English Language.* New York: Harcourt, Brace and World.

> A bit outdated but still a useful and readable introduction to the topic.

Sapir, Edward. 1921. *Language.* New York: Harcourt, Brace and Company.

> An enduring classic by one of the great linguists.

Serjeantson, Mary S. 1935. *A History of Foreign Words in English.* London: Routledge & Kegan Paul.

> This classic is still the best reference guide to the foreign words that have entered English.

Dictionaries

Borror, Donald J. 1960. *Dictionary of Word Roots and Combining Forms.* Palo Alto, California: N-P Publications.

> I have an old copy of this slender little book that my dad used in college, which I have laminated and carried with me on all of my hikes for nearly twenty years. I use it to look up the origins of every name, word, or technical term

that crosses my mind. It is the foremost book I would recommend to language-making students because it can be taken into the field and used as a living text.

Bosworth, Joseph, and T. Northcote Toller. 1898. *An Anglo-Saxon Dictionary*. Oxford: Oxford University Press.

Bosworth and Toller is still the only complete reference to Old English, though it is being supplanted by the forthcoming *Dictionary of Old English*, which is being published by the Pontifical Institute of Mediaeval Studies in Toronto (www.doe.utoronto.ca).

Jaeger, Edmund. 1955. *A Sourcebook of Biological Names and Terms*. Springfield, Illinois: Charles C. Thomas.

An essential handbook to the full range of elements (mostly Greek and Latin) that have gone into forming scientific words. Unfortunately, Jaeger's emphasis was on technical terminology, so many of the elements will be of limited use for a general vocabulary.

Kennedy, John. 1971. *A Stem Dictionary of the English Language*. Detroit, Michigan: Gale.

A quirky and casual arrangement but still a useful tool for understanding the close relationships of some words.

Kurath, Hans, and Sherman Kuhn. 1954. *Middle English Dictionary*. Ann Arbor: University of Michigan Press.

This massive dictionary (15,000 pages) reveals what might be the most amazing and productive period in the entire history of English. *Middle English* refers to the time when English was growing at a phenomenal rate, with so many words coming into the language that there were no formal spellings or correct forms—creating a confusing, exhilarating, and totally inspiring mix of words. The printed dictionary is very expensive and hard to find, but fortunately it is now available online (quod.lib.umich.edu/m/med).

Simpson, J. A., and E. S. C. Weiner. 1989. *The Oxford English Dictionary*. Oxford: Clarendon Press.

What is there that has not already been said about the OED? This is the definitive guide to the English lexicon, complete with extensive histories of each word. The publisher is working on an online version of a new third edition (www.oed.com), or you can track down a printed copy of the second edition.

Stone, Louise, and William Rothwell. 1977. *Anglo-Norman Dictionary*. London: Modern Humanities Research Association.

Anglo-Norman (Anglo-French) has had a profound influence on the English language, but without a specialized dictionary like this it is very difficult to appreciate the full range of Anglo-Norman words that have become part of Modern English. The print dictionary is almost impossible to find, and while the online version (www.anglo-norman. net) is now readily accessible and has been significantly updated, it is less satisfying to use.

Story, G. M., et al. 1990. *Dictionary of Newfoundland English*. Toronto: University of Toronto Press.

This dictionary might seem like an odd choice, but Newfoundland English may be the only living form of English that maintains a strong and vibrant connection to its old roots and to the land.

Urdang, Laurence. 1982. *Suffixes and Other Word-Final Elements of English*. Detroit, Michigan: Gale.

An essential compilation of all the suffixes that occur in English.

Urdang, Laurence. 1984. *Prefixes and Other Word-Initial Elements of English*. Detroit, Michigan: Gale.

An essential compilation of all the prefixes that occur in English.

Watkins, Calvert. 2011. *American Heritage Dictionary of Indo-European Roots*. Boston: Houghton Mifflin Harcourt.

For the English-speaking world, this is the only definitive guide to the roots that predate English, Latin, and Greek words, making it an absolutely vital reference for tracing the lineages and relationships of words.

Wright, Joseph. Reprinted 1962. *The English Dialect Dictionary*. New York: Hacker Art Books.

It is hard to know what to do with this amazing six-volume dictionary. As with Newfoundland English (a close cousin), these dialectical words from the English countryside sparkle with a sense of nature and rural life, but many of the words feel like outdated colloquialisms that lack any history and have no future. Still, it is a rich resource for anyone who wants to dive into these astonishing words, and I hope that someone does.

"Languages today are thin and cold because we think less and less into them. We are forced, for the sake of quickness and sharpness, to file down each word to its narrowest edge of meaning."

—Ernest Fenollosa, *The Chinese Written Character as a Medium for Poetry*

"The limits of my language are the limits of my world."

—Ludwig Wittgenstein

IN A NATURE REGISTER

CONSIDER THE WAYS you would speak and use words if you were sitting at a formal dinner with distinguished guests compared to hanging out with friends in a pub. This difference, whether it appears in speaking or writing, is called *register*, and it reflects how people tailor their words for different social settings, for the needs of their profession, or to convey an attitude or point of view.

Over time, the sum total of many instantaneous, highly specific decisions about what constitutes a particular register end up shaping language by codifying the use of some words while discouraging the use of other words. Registers can result in the formation of regional or social dialects, and they can even add new words to a language. Consider, for example, the massive influx of French words into the English language after the Norman Conquest, when exotic French words began to signal the development of a new "refined" register in place of the "uncouth" register of native English (Anglo-Saxon) words.

So if there are registers for formal social events; if there are registers for doctors, lawyers, and blue-collar workers; and if there are registers for urban youth; then why can't we create a "nature register"?

Other people might have different ideas, but I would suggest that a nature register could be composed of solid, earthy words drawn from English's Anglo-Saxon roots. I cannot imagine abstract Latinate words like *explicate* or *exemplify* being part of this register, though a sprinkling of lovely nature names could still be drawn from the classical tradition. And then this mix might be further enlivened with some of the playful punctuations and word-experiments explored in this book.

The result would be an earthy, classy, and experimental but carefully considered vocabulary for speaking of the natural world and our experiences in the natural world. It might be a register that mirrors nature in being unruly and trailless; it might even be prickly at times. But a register is never an individual creation, it is always a social phenomenon, so exactly how this looks can only be determined by those who create the register and use it.

❧

A large number of grammatical rules stem from arbitrary decisions that were made by early grammarians but lack any solid basis in the English language.

❧

CAPITAL IDEAS

DURING THE MANY years I spent writing articles for magazines and newspapers, I often found myself arguing with editors over their insistence on using lowercase letters for animal names. It was always my feeling that we should honor animals by capitalizing their names in the same way we capitalize other proper names. Furthermore, we often introduce unnecessary ambiguity when we use lowercase letters for animal names (for example, *the yellow warbler* could be either a species named "yellow warbler" or a warbler that is yellow).

There have been times when animal names would have been

capitalized (e.g., White-tailed Deer instead of white-tailed deer). In fact, until the late 1700s it was common practice to capitalize all, or nearly all, nouns—a practice that English once shared with German. Grammarians and printing companies led a push to stop capitalizing nouns (except in proper names), but even in the twenty-first century there is still lingering confusion about whether some nouns should be capitalized. For instance, it is not clear whether words like *national park, sun, moon*, or *heaven* should be capitalized.

People who write bird books tend to capitalize bird names but not the names of insects, fish, amphibians, reptiles, or mammals. And at the same time, plant names are not capitalized unless a plant is named after a specific person. It is a messy situation, and sadly the goal of speaking honorably about plants and animals never seems to be part of the debate.

In the late 1700s Benjamin Franklin complained bitterly about what was at that time the new trend of dropping capitals. Why did he staunchly defend the old practice of capitalizing nouns, and what would it be like to begin capitalizing nouns again? As Franklin pointed out, capitalized nouns help clarify expression, especially because English has a tendency to convert words into different parts of speech. We readily change the noun *table* into the verb *table* and vice versa, so it makes some sense to capitalize nouns like *Table* to distinguish them from their equivalent verb forms.

Or, as an alternative, we could radically transform the noun-heavy tone of English by capitalizing verbs instead, shifting our attention from things and objects to relationships and actions—

> not a fish can Leap or an insect Fall on the pond but it
> is thus Reported in circling dimples, in lines of beauty,
> as it were the constant Welling up of its fountain, the
> gentle Pulsing of its life, the Heaving of its breast.
> (Adapted from Thoreau's *Walden*)

Such a transformation from noun emphasis to verb emphasis is not entirely trivial, because the anthropologist Benjamin Lee Whorf suggested in the 1930s that a user's perception of time and space is profoundly altered in verb-rich languages such as the Hopi language. No matter whether we want to change our perception of time and space or simply honor the plants and animals of our world, it is a good exercise to consider adding capital letters to your writer's toolkit.

§a.

"The maintenance of standard language depends on obedience to authority … [and] some groups have more authority than others."
—James and Lesley Milroy

§a.

ANY NONCE SENSE?

DOES IT MAKE ANY SENSE to create words on the spur of the moment to address special or immediate needs? Such words are called *nonce words* (or more technically, *hapax legomenon*) if they are invented and used on a single occasion to meet a particular need. Nonce words usually don't enter the lexicon, so they might be dismissed as nonsense words, but at the same time they are one answer to the question of how to introduce words or processes to a language.

Perhaps more than any other writer, Chaucer used nonce words to great effect during the highly formative period when English emerged from Anglo-Norman occupation and began radically growing and stretching in new directions in the fourteenth century. Chaucer has even been credited with inventing "literary English" because he brought phenomenal energy and ingenuity to the very difficult task of creating a literary language by translating much-needed foreign words into English (which had lost its own native literary terms during centuries of occupation). He experimented tirelessly and fearlessly with unique forms of words, and then he readily dropped experimental words as soon as he created them in order to make room for even more words. It is important to realize that Chaucer's nonce creations were not imaginary nonsense words; they were thoughtful and serious attempts to convert foreign words and ideas into English words and ideas in the absence of models.

There is a lot of room for extraordinary innovation if there are no expectations that a word will be used a second time, and it is this freedom that Chaucer exploited so fruitfully in his experiments at translating foreign words into English. We can say fruitfully because many of Chaucer's experiments survived as a permanent part of the language, and he ended up having a profound influence on the shape and direction that English took as it evolved into Middle English and later into Modern English.

I take Chaucer as a model for why we should be fearless in experimenting with language, and it helps to realize that much of Chaucer's formative energy went into creating nonce words. You too can create nonce words: perhaps in the hope that other people will use your creations, or as a kind of "performance" of your language-making talents, or just because it's fun to play with language.

❦

A huge number of word experiments will (and should) fall by the wayside, but that is the essential nature of a vibrant language.

❦

CONTRACTION

WE HAVE ONE SURVIVING FRAGMENT of Sappho's poetry in which a line with a verb meaning 'to raise' is followed by a line with the same verb contracted to form a new word that means 'springtime.' It is as if, following this same example, we took *to raise* and contracted it into *to-ra* as a way of suggesting springtime—something like "to raise springtime to-ra." *To-ra* would not mean springtime to us at first glance, but this process might still be one provocative way to create new words from preexisting material.

❦

When language breaks open, what do we have left and what does it feel like?

❦

INTRODUCING NEOLOGISMS

INTRODUCING NEW WORDS to a language can be a tricky business, sure to elicit resistance or even scorn from entrenched experts ready to defend the integrity of "their" language. However, one successful tactic might be borrowed from Sir Thomas Elyot, a largely forgotten pioneer of Modern English who in the early 1500s wrote one of the first books of prose easily recognized as Modern English.

Elyot is credited with introducing many new words (*neologisms*) into the English language. Remarkably, a large number of the words he created or borrowed from classical languages have persisted, in large part because he was smart enough to imitate a Middle English technique for presenting new words.

Elyot's strategy was to pair up newly crafted words alongside words or phrases that were already well known, essentially placing his words in a familiar context and defining them from the moment he introduced them. For example, he presented the following new (and now common) words with italics in these pairings: "*animate* and give courage," "*education* or bringing up noble children," "*persist* and continue" (examples from Miller, *External Influences on English* and Hughes, *A History of English Words*).

Providing his readers with an immediate sense of familiarity proved to be an enormously successful tool for Elyot—as it might be for anyone creating new words. The basic task is to position a new or modified word, or word element, alongside a dictionary-like definition or clarification of what the neologism signifies.

Pairings could also be presented as appositions (in the sentence "This is my friend Bill" *Bill* is an appositive which helps clarify *my friend*) or as compound words (in the word *maidservant* either *maid* or *servant* could introduce and help define the other word of the compound). Both of these techniques can be used to place two elements alongside each other, which is what Elyot was trying to do as well.

Keep these tactics in mind as you create new words and see if they can help make strange new words look more familiar:

> Her cheeks shone *kupfiro* like copper and fire; these flowers *solbrite* with sunlight; in the *apiston* or beehive; we held together in our community of *EachOtherance*.

§

Prescriptivism: *"the view that one variety of a language has an inherently higher value than others and ought to be the norm for the whole speech community."*
—David Crystal, *The Cambridge Encyclopedia of the English Language*

"The ideology of prescriptivism [is], at base, driven by commercial interests."
—Richard Watts, *Language Myths and the History of English*

§

POP NATURE

AFTER READING AN ARTICLE about Andy Warhol and pop art one day, I suddenly realized that nature field guides are a kind of pop art—field guides simply represent reality in the same way that Warhol presented everyday utilitarian objects (for instance, Campbell's soup cans) as art that offered no pretense of interpretation.

The more I thought about it, the more I realized that field guides differ very little from other pop culture products such as mail-order catalogues. They are all artfully designed, attractively packaged, easy to consume, and ultimately intended to generate profit for some person or company.

Field guides may play a vital role in translating complex scientific information into pleasant little sound bites for a mass audience, but they also mirror and contribute to a culture that is losing sight of the many incredible ways nature can be interpreted. Field guides make all of us forget that there are (and should be) other unique visions of the natural world. I long to see a new generation of field guides that go beyond pop art, field guides that innovate and explore radically different traditions and styles as diverse as abstract expressionism or cubism in the arts.

ℬ

Advertising is "verbal theft of the property of the speech community."

ℬ

WORD ART

THERE ARE entire industries built around the *combination* of words—into sentences, stories, and poems—by writers and by the critics who analyze those works. At the same time, the *presentation* of words has been enormously elaborated by typesetters who have named and accentuated every feature of a text, from the sizes of margins to the dimensions of spaces between individual letters. But in the midst of all this professionalism it feels as if we have lost the art of the word itself.

Most people seem to assume that words appear, perfectly formed, out of thin air or from the mists of some vaguely perceived past and then those words are shifted around in clever ways to create lyrics, poems, and stories. While the combination and presentation of these predetermined words have become highly refined skills, the art of creating the words themselves seems to be missing, and this is an astonishing gap.

Why are word-making processes not thought of in the same ways that artists approach clay or paint, with the perspective that individual words and word elements are as malleable and dynamic as works of art? And if individual words were created from scratch in art-like ways, then imagine the creative potential of writers striving to shape the most beautiful and evocative words. What if there were writers who committed themselves to the sole craft of word creation? What if some words were admired for their artistic virtuosity rather than their function? What if you could attend a gallery opening to view uniquely crafted words on display?

Words could then be seen as shapely creations, with the result that some might inspire new ideas about meaning and representation, while others might be imitated or lifted wholesale into popular usage. Connoisseurs could recognize and discuss the subtle nuances of origin, or the internal plays on sound and structure. Is that word element drawn from Chaucer, for instance, or has that Anglo-Saxon element been merged with an Italian element? A gallery showing would not even have to be limited to individually crafted words; a presentation of new word-making rules, or groupings of words that illustrate imaginative linguistic structures or processes, could be pleasing creations too.

As a musician endlessly practices scales, why couldn't a word-maker practice processes of word-formation?

—*Sequences of word elements.*
—*Sequences of prefixes and suffixes.*
—*Sequences of letter and
sound shifts.*

A(F)-FIX-ING WORDS

ONE OF THE most important and productive language-making processes in English is affixation, the process by which we add prefixes and suffixes to words and word roots. Affixes are elements of grammar smaller than words. They cannot stand alone; they are usually added before (prefixes) or after (suffixes) words to modify meaning or create new words. Thus, the word *enjoyment* is formed by first adding the prefix *en-* to the base word *joy*, then adding the suffix *-ment* to the word *enjoy*. In this case the prefix converts a noun (*joy*) into a verb (*enjoy*), while the suffix converts the verb (*enjoy*) into a new noun (*enjoyment*) with a subtly different meaning than the original noun.

The process of compounding (that is, combining two words, as in *horsetail*) may be equally productive, but it is hard to describe this process because you could theoretically create almost any kind of word combination. On the other hand, there is a rather manageable set of affixes in English (on the order of several hundred), so it is far easier to list these affixes and begin experimenting with them. In fact, a list of affixes may end up being the single most important item in your language-making toolkit.

On the flip side, affixation is often a fairly trivial language-making process. By trivial I mean that no one is going to sit up and take notice if you add the suffix *-ish* to the base word *rock* to form the word *rockish* (whether this is a new word or not). This is not necessarily a drawback, but it is something to keep in mind if your goal is to push language toward new frontiers.

To this end it might help to consider a stepwise approach to thinking about affixation. The first, and easiest, step is to create words by adding standard affixes (the ones listed in any grammar or language book) to standard base words: *tree-ify, rock-ish*. A more complex step would be to add standard affixes to less familiar bases, in this case replacing *tree* and *rock* with unexpected classical bases: *arb-ify, lith-ish*. Next you could replace standard affixes with unusual affixes: *arb-isc, lith-dom*. And finally, you could reach into your imagination for metaphoric combinations not suggested by standard language-making rules: *treepil, duralith*. (Note that affixes readily undergo these kinds of metaphoric extensions and can even change meaning over time; for example, the prefix *meta-*, 'between, among,' later grew to include the added meaning 'exchanging or transferring' in words like *metamorphosis*.)

And this brings up a really important point: there are many books that list affixes, but in every example I have found these books list affixes that *have been* used in the formation of English. No one seems to list affixes that *could have been* used in English, and this means that many wonderful, exotic alternate forms have been left behind even though they have just as much potential to be productive as the affixes that were kept.

In the languages I have investigated closely—including Greek, Latin, Old English, and Anglo-Norman—there are numerous old affixes that have been preserved in the English we use today, but there are just as many affixes that were never transferred into English. And this is exactly where affixation starts to get exciting, because these neglected affixes offer language-making students an almost unlimited range of creative choices.

On top of this treasure trove of familiar and unfamiliar affixes, there is another component that few people think of: affixes often start out as freestanding words that through long association with other words gradually lose their independent existence. Therefore, a word like *rock*, which is currently productive in forming compound words such as *rockfall, rockslide, rock bottom, rock climbing*, and *rock and roll*, could over time be abbreviated to *roc* and used as an affix that implies the quality of something becoming solid. This is the same process that gave us the neoclassical combining form *geo-*, which started as the Greek word *ge*, 'land, earth,' and now conveys the quality of "belonging to earth" in words like *geology, geography*, and *geometry*.

The task, therefore, is to embrace affixation—already one of the most highly productive processes in English—and use it to take charge of creating imaginative new words through unique combinations, through the resurrection of old affixes, and through the shaping of new affixes. This is a lot to think about, so one starting point might be to build a list of basic affixes and then add to it over time as you encounter other interesting affixes (both old and new). For instance, I recently ran across a reference to an old suffix -*nos* (feminine)/-*na* (masculine), 'controller of, lord of,' which was used in ancient times to turn names into gods' names. I don't even remember which tradition this was part of, but it seemed like something that could be useful, so I added it to my toolkit.

Affixes are amazing. With just a few letters they carry so much tradition and meaning. The consistent application of suffixes, for example, has almost singlehandedly turned English into a poetic rhyming language, and many suffixes add such highly subtle shades of meaning that scholars have spent their entire lives studying these nuances.

Here then are some useful affixes. I have divided them in three ways: by origin, by function, and by property. These lists are far from complete, but I hope they encourage you to search for more affixes. The important thing to remember is that the affixes you find in dictionaries and language books are not endpoints; there are no limitations to the ways that affixes can be tweaked or created from scratch. I have tried to include alternate forms of affixes in some of the lists below to illustrate the many fluid ways that even standard affixes have changed over time.

Affixes by Origin

It is useful to divide affixes by origin because it helps us understand the unique contributions of different languages and because the act of combining affixes from one language with base words from another language is often frowned upon. Fortunately, so many words break this "rule" that it is not really worth worrying about, but you may still want to be aware of the origins of elements so you can consciously reinforce or counter expectations with each choice you make.

Many languages have contributed at least a few affixes to English, but our most important affixes can be divided into two major groups: those from native sources (mainly Germanic) and those from classical sources. For the purposes of this book I will focus on native affixes as expressed in Old English and classical affixes as they come to us through Greek and Latin. It is particularly challenging to trace the classical affixes because many Greek affixes were filtered through Latin and Old French (or other Romance languages) before settling into English, and they often took many forms during this long journey.

The other confusing thing about classical affixes is that in modern times there has been a tremendous resurgence of interest in Greek and Latin elements, with the result that many elements have been used as if they were traditional affixes when in fact they are modern inventions (properly called *neoclassical combining forms*). This highly productive process of creating new affixes is exactly the point of this book, but for the moment my preference is to focus on traditional affixes because their long history offers a depth and richness of possibility that is often lacking in neoclassical combining forms.

By way of illustration, the Greek suffix *-izō* (now written *-ize*) has been phenomenally productive in creating verbs with an astounding range of meanings, including 'to subject someone (or something) to something,' and 'to act upon, or to engage in an activity.' In contrast, neoclassical combining forms have rather limited meanings; for example, *bio-* ('life'), *geo-* ('earth'), *cardi-* ('heart'), *pseudo-* ('false'), and *photo-* ('light'). For a full listing of combining forms I recommend that you consult a specialized dictionary like Jaeger's *Sourcebook of Biological Names and Terms* or Urdang's *Prefixes and Other Word-Initial Elements of English*.

Affixes of Greek Origin

The following list includes original Greek affixes as well as Greek words (mostly prepositions) that were converted into combining forms either in classical times or in modern times. The difference between affixes and combining forms is very subtle and matters more to experts than anyone else, but the way to tell them apart is that an affix cannot combine with another affix to form a word (*pre-ish*), while a combining form can combine with another combining form to make a word (*geo-logy*). As you can see from the list below, it does not matter too much whether something is an affix or a combining form because both are very productive in creating new words.

a-/an- 'not, without, devoid of'

> Other forms: *in-* (Latin); *en-* (Middle English; also, *il-* [before *l*], *im-* [before *b, m, p*], *ir-* [before *r*], *i-* [before *gn*], and *jn-*); *un-* (English). Examples: *amorphous, anarchy.*

ant-/anti- 'before, against, opposing'

> Other forms: *anth-* (Greek); *ante-* (Latin); *antee-* (Anglo-Norman). Examples: *Antarctica, antithesis.*

di-/dia- 'through, across, apart'

> Closely related to *di-* 'two' (Greek); *di-/dif-/dir-/dis-* 'separate, apart' (Latin); *to-* 'separation' (Old English); *des-* 'not' (Anglo-Norman). May have evolved from *dus-* 'apart, wrong' (see *dys-* below). Examples: *diagonal, dihedral.*

dys- 'bad, faulty, ill'

> Derived from *dus-* 'apart, wrong' (Indo-European). Examples: *dysfunction, dyslexia.*

ep-/eph-/epi- 'on it, at it, towards it'

> Related to *api-* 'beside, near' (Sanskrit); *ob-* 'towards, facing' (Latin, see below). Examples: *epode, ephemeral, epicenter.*

hyper- 'over, above, beyond the ordinary'

Other forms: *upari* (Sanskrit); *huper-* (Greek); *super-* (Latin). Examples: *hyperactive, hypertension.*

meta- 'between, among; changing or exchanging'

Closely related to words meaning "in the middle": *madhya* (Sanskrit); *mesos* (Greek); *medius* (Latin); *mit* (Old High German); *middle/myde* (Middle English); *mid* (English). Examples: *metamorphosis, metaphysics.*

pro- 'before, to the front; for, in preparation for'

Other forms: *por-/prae-/pre-/primi-* (Latin); *pour-/pur-* (Old French); *fir-* (Old High German); *fore-/forth-* (Old English). Examples: *probiotic, profound.*

syn- 'together with'

Other forms: *syl-* (before *l*), *sym-* (before *b, m, p*), *sys-* (before *s*); previous forms *sun-* and *xun-*. Examples: *syllable, symmetry, synchronous, system.*

-ac 'belonging to; someone who suffers from or is impacted by a condition'

Other forms: *-ake/-akon/-akos/-iac* (Greek); *-acus* (Latin); *-ack/-acque* (Early Modern English). Often combined with *-al* (e.g., *demon-iac* and *demon-iac-al*). Examples: *aphrodisiac, hypochondriac.*

-asm 'the result or condition of an action'

Closely related to *-ism* and a large complex of *-ize* suffixes (see below), also related to *-astic*. Other forms: *-asma/-asmus* (Latin); *-asme* (French). Examples: *enthusiasm, spasm.*

-cy 'a state or condition indicated by the root word'

Often combined with other suffixes to form compound suffixes in the model of *-acy, -ancy, - cracy, -ency, -mancy*; equivalent in meaning to the native suffixes *-hood, -ship.*

Other forms: *-keia/-kia/-teia/-tia* (Greek); *-cia/-tia* (Latin); *-tie* (Old French). Examples: *infancy, secrecy.*

-*ess* 'status or position held by a female'

Other forms: *-issa* (Greek); *-esse* (Old French). Examples: *goddess, poetess.*

-*ic* 'belonging to, connected with, characteristic of'

One of the most productive suffixes in Greek, plus it has readily combined with other suffixes to produce compound suffixes in the pattern of *-atic, -etic, -ical, -ically, -icly, -icate, -ication, -ician, -icism, -icist, -icity, -icize, -icose, -icular, -icule, -istic, -itic.* Other forms: *-ikos* (Greek); *-icus* (Latin); *-ique* (Old French); *-ike/-ick/-yke* (Middle English); by way of illustration consider the historic sequence *angelikos* (Greek), *angelicus* (Latin), *angelique* (French), *angelick/angelyke* (Middle English), *angelic* (English). Examples: *magic, rustic.*

-*ise/-ize* 'to act upon, engage in'

A highly productive suffix in English (at least formerly); closely related to *-ism/-ist,* compare for instance *baptize/ baptism/baptist.* Other forms: *-izein* (Greek); *-izare* (Latin); *-iser* (Old French); *-isen* (Middle English). Examples: *botanize, naturalize.*

-*sis* 'a result, process, or action (of the verb)'

Related to *-sic/-tic* and combined with other suffixes to form suffixes such as *-asis, -esis, -iasis, -lysis, -osis.* Examples: *analysis, symbiosis.*

Affixes of Latin Origin

Latin affixes have been extremely productive in English, and a phenomenal variety of Latin affixes are by now so familiar to English speakers that few people recognize these elements as "borrowed." The list of suffixes alone is so extensive they are the subject of a fascinating book (*Latin Suffixal*

Derivatives in English and Their Indo-European Ancestry by D. Gary Miller). These affixes are used by English speakers to create or understand new words on an almost daily basis, and a full command of them will go a long ways toward enhancing your own language-making skills. I cannot list all of these affixes in this book, but here is a sampling of some useful Latin affixes.

ad- 'to, toward'

> When followed by *b, c, f, g, l, n, p, r, s*, or *t* changes to *ab-, ac-, af-, ag-, al-, an-, ap-, ar-, as-* or *at-*; reduced to *a-* when followed by *sc, sp*, or *st*. Examples: *accept, address, announce, aspire, attack, aspect.*

com- 'with, together'

> Other forms: *co-* before vowels (*coauthor, cooperate*) and often before *h* (*cohere*) or *w* (*coworker*); *con-* before *c, d, f, g, j, k, n, s, t, v*, and often before *n* (*connect*). Examples: *combine, compel, contact, convey.*

de- 'from, away from, a result of'

> Closely related to *di(a)-* (see above), including *di-/dif-/dir-/dis-/des-*. Examples: *decode, destabilize.*

in- 'in, within, toward; not'

> Other forms: *il-* (before *l*), *im-* (before *b, m, p*), *ir-* (before *r*); *en-* (French). In the sense of 'not,' it is synonymous with and competes with native English *un-* (as in pairs like *inhuman/unhuman*). Examples: *invade, illogical, imprison, irrespective, engulf.*

ob- 'toward, against; upon, over; completely'

> Related to *api-* (Sanskrit); *epi-* (Greek). Other forms: *oc-* (before *c*), *of-* (before *f*), *o-* (before *m*), *op-* (before *p*). Examples: *object, occasion, offend, omit, opponent.*

re- 'back to an original place, again'

Formerly *red-* before vowels (as in *redemption*); closely related form is *retro-*, which is built on the same model as *intro-* (*in+ter+o-*) and *extro-* (*ex+ter+o-*). Also obscurely hidden in a few words of French origin (e.g., *rally, ransom*). Examples: *regenerate, renew.*

sub- 'under, inferior to'

Closely related to *upa-* (Sanskrit) and *hupo-* (Greek). Other forms: *suc-* (before *c*), *suf-* (before *f*), *sug-* (before *g*), *sum-* (before *m*), *sup-* (before *p*), *sur-* (before *r*), and sometimes *sus-* (before *c, p*, and *t*). Examples: *subject, succeed, suffice, suggest, summon, supplant, surreal, susceptible, suspend, sustain.*

-al 'characterized by, belonging to'

The Latin form *-alis* is derived from the combination of *-a-* plus the suffix *-li-* (which adds a sense of relationship). Note that *-alis* changes to *-aris* (Latin) and *-ar* (English) if the stem word already contains an *l* (e.g., *angle* becomes *angular* instead of *angulal*). Other forms: *-alia/ -ilia* (Latin); *-aille* (Old French); *-ail/-aile/-aylle* (Middle English). Readily combines with other suffixes to form *-ality, -alization, -alize, -ally, -ial, -ical, -oidal, -orial, -ual*. Examples: *floral, local.*

-an 'belonging to, from or characteristic of'; later also meaning 'a specialist in, follower of'

Related to *-inus* (Latin) and *-ine* (English, e.g., *alpine*). Other forms: *-anum/-anus/-ianus* (Latin); *-ain/-aigne/ -ayne/-en* (Old French); *-ano* (Italian and Spanish); *-an/ -ana/-ane/-ian* (English). Examples: *American/Americana, human/humane, musician.*

-ary 'thing or person connected with; place for something'

This large and highly productive group of affixes derives from Latin *-aria/-arium/-arius*. Other forms: *-aire/ -ariel/-ier/-iere* (Old French); *-arie/-arye/-erie* (Middle

English); *-iera/-iere/-iero* (Italian); *-arian/-arious/-arium/-er/-ery* (English). Examples: *solitary, agrarian, gregarious, terrarium, grocer/grocery.*

-ble 'suitable for, tending to'

This was one of the most productive affixes in Anglo-Norman, and many words entered Middle English with this affix; it continues to be productive in the creation of new English words. Other forms: *-abilis/-ebilis/-ibilis/-ubilis* (Latin); *-able/-ability/-ible/-ibility/-uble/-ubility* (English; note that *-eble/-ebility* forms are possible but archaic and now replaced by *-ible/-ibility*). Examples: *capable/capability, eligible/eligibility, soluble/solubility.*

-id 'result, state'

Formerly productive in French (where most English words with this suffix come from) but does not form new words in English at this time. Other forms: *-idem/-idus/-is* (Latin); *-ide* (Old French). Examples: *arid, fluid.*

-itude/-tude 'a state or condition, especially an observable state'

Meaning and usage closely parallels the native English *-ness* (see also *-ity* below). Other forms: *-itudin/-tudin/-itudo/-tudo* (Latin); *-itud/-tud* (Spanish). Examples: *gratitude, longitudinal.*

-ity/-ty 'state or condition'

Productive in Old French (found on French words borrowed by Chaucer, for instance) but has lost ground to native English *-ness* in modern times. Can be combined with *-al, -ble, -id* and other suffixes (e.g., *locality, ability, fluidity*). Other forms: *-etas/-itas/-tas* (Latin); *-ite/-itee/-te/-tee* (Anglo-Norman). Examples: *activity, liberty.*

-ment 'result, means'

Frequently co-occurs with *be-* (*bewilderment*), *em-* (*embankment*), *en-* (*enjoyment*), and *-ish* (*nourishment*).

Other forms: *-men/-mentum* (Latin). Examples: *abdomen, regimen/regiment, filament, moment/momentum.*

-ole 'small one'

The Indo-European element *-lo-* informed a range of Latin suffixes referring to small or diminutive things including *-cula/-culum/-culus, -ella/-ellis/-ellum, -illa/-illum/-illus, -ola/-olum/-olus, -ula/-ulum/-ulus*; these have in turn informed English suffixes such as *-cle, -cule, -el/-le, -ellum, -il, -illa, -ole, -ule.* Other forms: *-aglio/-iglio, -ola/-olo, -ula/-ulo* (Italian); *-eil/-eille* (French). Examples: *muscle, ridicule, mussel, castle, flagellum, pupil, scintilla, vacuole, rivulet.*

-ose/-ous 'full of, of the nature of'

Can be combined with *-ity* to form nouns (*porous* → *porosity*); also used in rendering a wide range of Latin suffixes (including *-aci, -ax, -endus, -er, -eus, -ius, -oci, -orus, -ox, -ris, -uus, -vorus*) into "English" forms (for example *-aceus, -acious, -orious, -uous*). Other forms: *-osa/-osum/-osus* (Latin); *-os* (Old French); *-eus/-euse/-eux* (French); occasionally *-us* (English; e.g., *cirrus, mucus, sinus*). Note that similar-looking *-eous* probably derives from Latin *-eus* rather than *-ous*. Examples: *morose, glorious.*

-tion 'event, result'

Very productive suffix in English; originally formed from the combination of *-t-* with the suffix *-ion*, then later combining with *-ate, -ify, -ize* to form compound suffixes *-ation, -ification, -ization.* Has the same meaning as the native English suffix *-ing* (compare for instance the borrowed Latin word *education* vs. the native Old English word *learning*). Other forms: *-io/-ion/-sio/-sion/-tio* (Latin); *-acioun/-cion/-cioun/-ciun* (Anglo-Norman). Examples: *action, elevation, passion.*

-tive/-sive 'relating to, characterized by'

Formed from the combination of *-t-* with the suffix *-ive*;

63

and combined with other elements to produce *-ative,
-itive, -ivity*. Other forms: *-ivus/-sivus/-tivus* (Latin);
-if/-ive (Old French; note that a few French words
dropped the *f*, creating words with *i* [=*y*] endings, e.g.,
hasty, jolly, tardy); *-ivo* (Italian). Examples: *native, pensive,
propulsive*; also *bailiff*, *naif* (from Old French).

-tor/-sor/-trice/-trix 'an agent, actor'

This highly productive suffix in Latin also combined with
-ius to form another very large group of compound suffixes
in the pattern of *-torius/-sorius/-orius* (equaling *-tory/-sory*
in English). Other forms: *-ator* (Latin); feminine forms
-trice/-trix are rare in English (e.g., *dominatrix*). Examples:
doctor, professor, predator.

Affixes of English Origin

Old English affixes often competed with classical affixes, a
situation in which one form triumphed over the other or else
both survived by taking on slightly different meanings. Old
English affixes are a strange mix to a modern speaker. The affixes are either very familiar (e.g., *-dom* in *wisdom*) or totally
alien (e.g., *-isc* in *Englisc* 'English'). And there are usually no alternate forms of these affixes, because they did not go through
the filter of intervening languages between Old English and
Modern English (compared to Greek and Latin affixes, which
were often filtered through intervening languages for hundreds
of years before arriving in English).

Sadly, a large number of Old English affixes have been
lost or abandoned through competition with classical affixes,
and some of the most interesting work we could do with the
English language is to give these old affixes new life (and also
new forms). To this end I have included more Old English affixes than classical affixes, and in the following list I have also
included examples of how it might look to create new words
with these old affixes.

a- used with verbs to intensify action (*bītan* 'to bite' vs. *abītan* 'to devour'); can also change a verb from habitual or continuous action to momentary action (*fysan* 'make haste' vs. *afysan* 'to hasten away'). Example: *run → arun* ('to race, run after').

æg- imparts indefinite meaning to pronouns and adverbs (*hwær* 'where' vs. *æghwær* 'everywhere'). Example: *tree → agtree* ('forestland').

and-/ond- usually signifies "against, opposite" (*sacan* 'to fight' vs. *andsacan* 'adversary'). Example: *deposit → ondeposit* ('erosion').

be-/bi- modifies verbs by adding sense of "about, around" (*gān* 'to go' vs. *begān* 'to go over, surround'); also added to some common adverbs and prepositions as in Modern English *before, behind, beneath, between*. Example: *feather → befeather* ('to cover in feathers').

ed- adds sense of "again, repetition" (*cennan* 'to create' vs. *edcennan* 'to regenerate'). Examples: *gust → edgust* ('storm'); *adjust → edjust* ('evolve').

el- suggests "foreignness, strangeness" (*land* 'land, earth' vs. *elland* 'a foreign country'). Example: *plant → elplant* ('introduced weed').

for- intensifies verbs (*bærnan* 'to burn' vs. *forbærnan* 'to burn up'); can also add "very" to adjectives and adverbs (*heard* 'hard' vs. *forheard* 'very hard'). Examples: *ate → forate* ('devoured'); *tall → fortall* ('towering').

fore- suggests "preeminence or precedence" (*gān* 'to go' vs. *foregān* 'to go before, precede'). Example: *sun → foresun* ('dawn').

forð- (=*forth-*) signals "forward motion" (*gang* 'going' vs. *forðgang* 'going forth, progress'). Example: *flow → forthflow* ('flowing outward').

ful-/full- intensifies meaning (*gān* 'to go' vs. *fulgān* 'accomplish'); or signals "completeness" (*growan* 'to grow' vs. *fullgrowan* 'to grow to perfection'). Example: *seed → fullseed* ('plant').

ge- added to verbs to indicate completed action or result; can also add a sense of collectiveness or completeness (*findian* 'to find' vs. *gefunden* 'found'). Example: *flower → geflower* ('flowered').

in- suggests the direction "in" (*gān* 'to go' vs. *ingān* 'to go into, to enter'); or intensifies the sense of the root word (*frōd* 'wise' vs. *infrōd* 'very wise'). Example: *burrow → inburrow* ('burrowing into').

mis- conveys sense of "amiss, wrongly" (*dæd* 'deed' vs. *misdæd* 'misdeed'). Example: *soil → missoil* ('ruined earth').

of- added to verbs to indicate completed or intensified action (*bēatan* 'to beat' vs. *ofbēatan* 'to beat to death'). Example: *fly → offly* ('to flee').

ofer- adds meaning of "over" to verbs (*helmian* 'to cover' vs. *oferhelmian* 'to overshadow'); or adds sense of "superiority" to verbs and other parts of speech (*cuman* 'to come' vs. *ofercuman* 'to overcome'). Examples: *sky → ofersky* ('heaven'); *branch → oferbranch* ('canopy').

on- used with verbs to indicate the start of an action (*stellan* 'to set or stand' vs. *onstellan* 'to institute or create'); can also reverse the root meaning of a verb (*bindan* 'to bind' vs. *onbindan* 'to unbind'), or convey the meaning "against, in reply to" (*ræs* 'violent rushing' vs. *onræs* 'to attack'). Example: *grow → ongrow* ('begin growing').

tō- adds basic meaning "to" (*gān* 'to go' vs. *tōgān* 'to go to'); can also indicate separation (*brecan* 'to break' vs. *tōbrecan* 'to break into pieces'). Examples: *fly → tofly* ('to fly to'); *stand → tostand* ('to stand apart').

þurh- (=*thurh-*) adds basic meaning of "through" (*brecan* 'to break' vs. *þurhbrecan* 'to break through'). Example: *climb → thruclimb* ('to climb through').

un- reverses the root meaning of a word (see *on-*).

under- adds basic meaning "under" (*flōwan* 'to flow' vs. *underflōwan* 'to flow under').

up- adds basic meaning "up" (*cuman* 'to come' vs. *upcuman* 'to arise').

ūt- adds basic meaning "out" (*land* 'land, earth' vs. *ūtland* 'outland, the countryside'). Example: *side* → *utside* ('outside').

wan-/won- indicates a negative or deprived sense (*hoga* 'thoughtful' vs. *wanhoga* 'thoughtless'). Example: *warm* → *wanwarm* ('chilled').

wið- (=*with-*) conveys sense of "against" (*suðan* 'in the south' vs. *wiðsuðan* 'to the south of'). Example: *hold* → *withhold* ('to hold back').

ymb(e)- adds basic meaning "around" (*sittan* 'to sit' vs. *ymbsittan* 'to beseige'). Example: *egg* → *imbegg* ('eggshell').

-bora turns nouns into agent nouns (*æsc* 'a spear made of ash' vs. *æscbora* 'spear-bearer'). Example: *wing* → *wingbora* ('a bird').

-cund adds the meaning "of the nature of" (*god* 'God' vs. *godcund* 'sacred'). Example: *earth* → *earthcund* ('home').

-dōm turns nouns or adjectives into abstract nouns (*wīs* 'wise' vs. *wīsdōm*). Example: *grass* → *grassdom* ('meadow').

-ed/-en turns nouns into adjectives (*hring* 'ring' vs. *hringed* 'made of rings, ringed'; *stan* 'stone' vs. *stænen* 'made of stones, stony'). Example: *grass* → *grassen* ('grassy').

-el forms nouns (*gyrde* 'to gird' vs. *gyrdel* 'a girdle'). Example: *lap* ('to drink') → *lapel* ('a drink').

-end forms agent nouns (indicating who is performing an action), sometimes with the meaning of *-er* (*hæl* 'to heal' vs. *hælend* 'healer'; *eard* 'home' vs. *eardiend* 'dweller'). Example: *wild* → *wildend* ('an inhabitant of the wild').

-ere forms agent nouns with basic meaning *-er* (*sang* 'song' vs. *sangere* 'singer'). Example: *bird* → *birdere* ('one who studies birds').

-hād turns concrete nouns into abstract nouns (*cild* 'child' vs. *cildhād* 'childhood'). Example: *altar* → *altarhad* ('divinity').

-ig usually turns nouns into adjectives (*blōd* 'blood' vs. *blōdig* 'bloody'). Example: *wood* → *woodig* ('woody').

-ing turns nouns and adjectives into concrete nouns with the meaning "derived from, associated with," thus often used to mean "son of" (*cyn* 'people or tribe' vs. *cyning* 'a king,' literally "son of the people"). Example: *peak* → *peaking* ('mountaintop').

-isc turns nouns into adjectives (*Engle* 'the people of Anglen [England]' vs. *Englisc* 'English'). Example: *bug* → *bugisc* ('buggish').

-lic turns adjectives and nouns into adjectives (*heofan* 'heaven' vs. *heofonlic* 'heavenly'). Example: *earth* → *earthlic* ('earthly').

-ling forms concrete nouns, often in a diminutive state (*dēore* 'dear' vs. *dēorling* 'darling'). Example: *star* → *starling* ('little star').

-nes(s) turns adjectives into abstract nouns (*beorht* 'bright' vs. *beorhtnes* 'brightness'). Example: *wide* → *widenes* ('width').

-scipe (equivalent to *-ship* in Modern English) turns nouns and adjectives into abstract nouns (*gōd* 'good' vs. *gōdscipe* 'goodness'). Example: *free* → *freescipe* ('freedom').

-ung/-ing forms abstract nouns (*leornian* 'to learn' vs. *leornung* 'learning'; *ræd* 'to read' vs. *ræding* 'reading'). Example: *flock* → *flockung* ('flocking').

Affixes by Function

Affixes may also be classified according to their capacity

to turn words into new parts of speech, as when *-ful* turns a noun into an adjective (*joy* → *joyful*). This is largely the role of suffixes, and very few prefixes (such as *a-, be-, en-*) perform this same grammatical function. In a case like *joyful* the function of the affix is fairly straightforward; it simply creates an adjective that means "full of joy." But in some cases the shift is more subtle; for example, most of us would be hard pressed to explain the difference between the noun *joy* and the noun *enjoyment* (a noun created through affixation).

Lists of affixes sorted by their functions are helpful because it is fun to play with other affixes that can perform the same function and see what you discover. For instance, *enjoyment* might (or might not) find parallel or alternate meanings if you swap out *-ment* for other noun-making affixes to form words such as *enjoyage, enjoyal, enjoyant, enjoyation, enjoyor*, etc. (though not all choices are available due to underlying usage rules). As you can see from the examples below, the meanings of these affixes are often vague and flexible enough that they can be loosely (hence "creatively") applied.

Making Nouns

-acy/-asy 'state or quality.' Examples: *aristocracy, idiosyncrasy*.

-age 'collective result, place of, agent of.' Examples: *foliage, passage, savage*.

-al 'act of, process of.' Examples: *arrival, revival*.

-an/-ian 'belonging to, skilled in.' Examples: *American, amphibian, magician*.

-ance/-ence 'quality or state.' Examples: *occurrence, radiance, substance*.

-ant/-ent 'one who performs an action.' Examples: *migrant, rodent*.

-ast 'one associated with.' Examples: *enthusiast, gymnast*.

-ation 'process or state of being acted upon, connected with

69

an action.' Examples: *contemplation, glaciation.*

-dom 'a realm, state of being.' Examples: *kingdom, wisdom.*

-eer 'an agent (often in a professional capacity).' Examples: *mountaineer, volunteer.*

-er 'an agent of, native of.' Examples: *forester, seeker.*

-ery/-ry 'abstract collectivity.' Examples: *fishery, nursery.*

-ess 'feminine agent.' Examples: *goddess, lioness.*

-ette 'a diminutive or female agent.' Examples: *brunette, kitchenette.*

-ful 'the quantity that fills.' Examples: *roomful, spoonful.*

-hood 'abstract state of.' Examples: *adulthood, neighborhood.*

-ia 'condition of.' Examples: *euphoria, mammalia, suburbia.*

-ing 'an action or result of an action.' Examples: *engraving, flying, hiking.*

-ism 'doctrine or set of beliefs, behavior characteristic of.' Examples: *alcoholism, Buddhism, paganism.*

-ist 'one who enacts an action, skill, or set of beliefs.' Examples: *aerialist, biologist, communist.*

-ity 'state or quality of.' Examples: *activity, biodiversity, curiosity.*

-let/-ling 'small one.' Examples: *auklet, booklet, duckling.*

-ment 'result of an action.' Examples: *agreement, sediment.*

-ness 'state or condition of.' Examples: *awareness, bitterness, holiness.*

-ship 'state or condition of.' Examples: *friendship, interrelationship.*

-ster 'one who makes or is associated with.' Examples: *songster, youngster.*

Making Verbs

-*ate* 'cause to happen.' Examples: *create, elevate, generate.*

-*en* 'cause to be.' Examples: *broken, darken, steepen.*

-*ify/-fy* 'cause to be, to make into.' Examples: *beautify, countrify, magnify.*

-*ize* 'cause to be, to become.' Examples: *crystallize, fossilize, hybridize.*

Making Adjectives

-*able/-ible/-uble* 'capable of, fit for.' Examples: *drinkable, edible, soluble.*

-*al/-ial/-ical/-ual* 'having the property of, relating to.' Examples: *global, glacial, geological, gradual.*

-*ary* 'of, or relating to.' Examples: *pituitary, sedimentary, tributary.*

-*ate* 'full of, having.' Examples: *desolate, passionate.*

-*ed* 'characterized by.' Examples: *forested, illuminated, watered.*

-*escent* 'becoming, beginning.' Examples: *acquiescent, crescent, iridescent.*

-*ese* 'native to, or belonging to a place.' Examples: *Chinese, officialese, Siamese.*

-*esque* 'in the manner or style of.' Examples: *grotesque, picturesque.*

-*ful* 'full of, having the qualities of.' Examples: *hopeful, restful, wonderful.*

-*ic* 'having the property or nature of.' Examples: *aerobic, biotic, cryptic.*

-*ish* 'inclined to, being like.' Examples: *hawkish, sheepish, toadish.*

-ive 'characterized by.' Examples: *cooperative, supportive, vegetative.*

-less 'without, not having.' Examples: *cloudless, endless, nameless.*

-ly 'having the appearance or manner of.' Examples: *chilly, daily, godly.*

-oid 'having the shape or appearance of.' Examples: *asteroid, deltoid, humanoid.*

-ory 'belonging to, connected with.' Examples: *olfactory, sensory.*

-ose 'full of, possessing the qualities of.' Examples: *cellulose, foliose, verbose.*

-ous 'possessing, abounding in.' Examples: *aqueous, poisonous, vigorous.*

-some 'characterized by.' Examples: *adventuresome, awesome, handsome.*

-y 'characterized by, full of.' Examples: *hairy, sandy, watery.*

Affixes by Property

While suffixes change the parts of speech and meanings of words, prefixes are valuable for the ways they modify the properties of words. "Properties" is a fairly vague term, and different authors have sorted prefixes into different categories; however, the intent of this book is not to offer firm categories but to highlight the fact that it is possible to group prefixes in meaningful ways. The categories I have chosen are quantity, location, time, negation, and miscellaneous. For example, the prefixes of negation are not necessarily related etymologically but have the common property of restricting, reversing, or negating the words they modify. These categories are useful because they illustrate how prefixes work, and in some cases the categories suggest prefixes that could be interchanged or used to signal slightly different meanings (compare *inhuman* vs. *unhuman*).

It is inspiring to realize that prefixation is a fluid and creative process and that a large number of prefixes have been invented in modern times (recall that these are more properly called neoclassical combining forms). For instance, the prefix *ecto-* was created from a Greek word and first used in the mid-1800s; it has since become productive in the formation of new technical and scientific words. Prefixes are also very fluid in attaching to almost any type of word (suffixes usually attach to words in one part of speech and convert them into words in another part of speech), and they can take on different forms to facilitate this process. For example, the prefix *ad-* readily changes its form depending on the first letter of the word it modifies (something that suffixes never do), with the option of turning into *a-*, *ac-*, *af-*, *ag-*, *al-*, *ap-*, *as-*, or *at-*. I have not attempted to include all these options in the lists below, but keep this fluidity in mind, because it is one of the reasons why prefixes are important creative tools.

Quantity Prefixes

a-/an- 'lacking, without.' Examples: *asymmetry, anarchy.*

bi-/di- 'two.' Examples: *bilateral, dioxide.*

demi-/hemi-/semi- 'half.' Examples: *demigod, hemisphere, semitranslucent.*

hyper-/over-/super- 'excessively.' Examples: *hyperactive, overachiever, superachiever.*

is-/iso- 'equal.' Examples: *isopod, isosceles.*

macro-/mega- 'large.' Examples: *macrophage, megalith.*

micro-/mini- 'small.' Examples: *microscopic, minimum.*

mono-/uni- 'one.' Examples: *monoceros, unicorn.*

multi-/poly- 'many.' Examples: *multiple, polygon.*

oligo- 'few.' Example: *oligarch.*

omni-/pan- 'all.' Examples: *omniscient, pantheism.*

tri- 'three.' Example: *tripod.*

under- 'insufficiently.' Example: *undernourished.*

Location Prefixes

ab-/apo-/de-/di-/dis- 'away, away from.' Examples: *abnormal, apocalypse, decline, digress, disregard.*

ad- 'toward' (other forms *a-, ac-, af-, ag-, al-, ap-, as-, at-*). Examples: *advance, affix.*

anti-/cata-/contra-/counter- 'against.' Examples: *antigravity, catastrophe, contrary, counterbalance.*

circum-/peri- 'around.' Examples: *circumference, perimeter.*

co-/con-/syn- 'together, jointly.' Examples: *coexist, confluence, synergy.*

dia-/tra-/trans-/tres- 'across.' Examples: *dialogue, tradition, transfer, trespass.*

ec-/ecto-/ex-/exo- 'external.' Examples: *ecstasy, ectoparasite, exterior, exoskeleton.*

en-/endo-/in-/intra- 'inside, internal.' Examples: *enclose, endocrine, inside, intravenous.*

epi-/super-/sur- 'over.' Examples: *epigram, superhuman, surfeit.*

fore-/pro- 'in front of, first.' Examples: *forearm, proceed.*

infra-/sub- 'below, within.' Examples: *infrared, subterranean.*

inter- 'between.' Examples: *interject, intersect.*

para- 'along with.' Examples: *paragraph, parallel.*

retro- 'back, backward.' Examples: *retroactive, retrospect.*

se- 'by itself, apart from.' Examples: *secede, separate.*

Time Prefixes

ante-/fore-/pre-/pro-/proto- 'before, preceding.' Examples: *antecedent, foregone, preposition, propose, prototype.*

ex- 'former.' Example: *ex-president.*

neo- 'new.' Examples: *neolithic, neonate.*

paleo- 'early.' Example: *paleolithic.*

post- 'after.' Example: *postpone.*

re-/red- 'again.' Examples: *return, redux.*

Negation Prefixes

a- 'without, not.' Examples: *asexual, asymmetrical.*

anti- 'against, opposite.' Examples: *anticlimax, antithesis.*

de- 'reversal, removal.' Examples: *deforest, defrost.*

dis- 'not.' Examples: *disagree, disqualify.*

in- 'not.' Examples: *inactive, indirect.*

mal- 'evil, not good.' Examples: *malformed, malnourish.*

mis- 'wrongly, badly.' Examples: *mistake, mistreat.*

non- 'not.' Examples: *nonhuman, nonnative.*

ob- 'opposite, in the way of.' Examples: *objection, oblivion.*

pseudo- 'not real, not true.' Examples: *pseudonym, pseudoscience.*

un- 'absence, removal, reversal.' Examples: *unnatural, undress, undo.*

Miscellaneous Prefixes

arch- 'chief, leader.' Examples: *archangel, archenemy.*

auto- 'self, native, natural.' Examples: *autobiography, autochthonic, autonomy.*

dys- 'bad.' Examples: *dysfunction, dyslexia.*

eu- 'good.' Examples: *eulogy, euphoria.*

hyper- 'above or beyond the ordinary.' Examples: *hyperactive, hyperbole.*

mero- 'part, portion.' Examples: *merogenesis, meronym.*

meta- 'changing, exchanging.' Examples: *metabolism, metamorphosis.*

proto- 'first.' Examples: *prototype, protozoa.*

ultra- 'beyond, extreme.' Examples: *ultraconservative, ultrasound.*

vice- 'to stand for, in place of.' Examples: *vice president, viceroy.*

There are hundreds of affixes to choose from (see the two books by Urdang, *Suffixes and Other Word-Final Elements of English* and *Prefixes and Other Word-Initial Elements of English*), and while some affixes aren't particularly interesting for a language-making student (e.g., *-like*), other affixes might be more interesting and productive (e.g., *-al*). Out of the hundreds of available affixes, the task is to find the affixes you can believe in; these might be the affixes that will be your go-to choices when creating words. Do you prefer affixes from certain origins? Do you favor noun-making affixes or verb-making affixes? Choices like these could become part of your signature style.

ॐ

4500 new words were added to the English language each decade from 1500 to 1700, and two-thirds of these words were created from existing roots and affixes.

ॐ

FOUR WAYS TO CREATE ORIGINAL WORDS

- Borrow and repurpose old words or change them into new words

- Add prefixes or suffixes to preexisting words

- Convert a word to a new part of speech

- Combine two or more words into a new compound word

❧

In a time of great crisis language is something that can lead us forward.

Bring every word to life:
—know its roots
—place it carefully
—have it mean
something.

❧

OLD ENGLISH:
BACK TO THE ROOTS

THE ENGLISH LANGUAGE we use today has changed so much over the past thousand years that it's almost impossible for a modern reader to understand Old English texts from 450–1100. In fact, some scholars even refer to this early language as Anglo-Saxon rather than Old English in recognition of how radically different it is from Modern English.

The English language first began to profoundly change with the invasion of elite French culture after the Norman Conquest of 1066, and then picked up steam during the Renaissance of the fourteenth through the seventeenth centuries when a great number of words and ideas were borrowed from classical literature. Newly adopted Greek, Latin, and French words conveyed so much prestige that native English words were judged uncouth in comparison and largely dropped from the vocabulary of the educated ruling classes.

In a way, it is true that native English words seem unrefined, but for unexpected reasons. Consider the Old English words that we still use in Modern English: they are nearly always short, single-syllable words that point to concrete objects, the "unsophisticated stuff" of everyday life such as *sun, moon, day, month, year, hand, eye, heart, home, house, door, land, field, wood, see, eat, sit, love, kiss, god, death, live.* This raw, earthy core of native words has been buried beneath an onslaught of abstract, multisyllable words from the classical tradition: vast numbers of words like *literature, justice, authority, exasperation, modesty, animation.* And once submerged, native words became "fossilized"—in other words, they stopped dynamically evolving and have remained frozen in their original form and meaning for at least a thousand years.

It is not too much of an exaggeration to say that the native word stock has been buried underneath an onslaught of foreign words; while 85 percent of the original Old English words have been dropped from the language, more than 70 percent of the words now used in Modern English have been borrowed from other languages (mostly Latin and French).

Although native English words now form a relatively small part of Modern English, it is notable that they comprise the most important words in our vocabulary. For example, virtually every one of the hundred most frequently used words in the English language is of native origin (the only exceptions are a few vital words, such as *they* and *are*, that were borrowed from Scandinavian a very long time ago).

The editors of *The Oxford English Dictionary* call these fundamental native words the "Common Words." Other authors refer to them as the "core vocabulary" or "base register" in recognition of the fact that these common words, despite a long history of ridicule, still form the essential skeleton around which the English language is built.

It is as if native words form the foundation and framework of a house, while all the later borrowings are ornaments, fixtures, windows, and other final touches. This "foundational" quality has led some thinkers astray, into an Anglo-centric belief that this older English is somehow more pure, more authentic, or more legitimate (for an extended analysis of this issue see *Language Myths and the History of English* by Richard Watts).

But it is more accurate to look at what really happened to Old English, because at the time of the Norman Conquest, Old English was "the most highly developed vernacular of Northern Europe." In an idea proposed by Derek Brewer and quoted in Christopher Cannon's book *The Making of Chaucer's*

English, this surprisingly advanced and subtle language was gutted by Norman invaders, who ruled England for 300 years and brought with them the language, literature, and culture of both French and classical traditions.

The pieces of Old English that survived this wave of invaders were the core words that illiterate peasants and villagers could not live without, and it is this basic fact that makes the native words that have survived in modern times feel so earthy and essential. As described by Brewer, Old English also had plenty of words for abstract ideas and aesthetic or literary values, but these "elevated" words were the ones that were discarded or replaced by foreign borrowings.

So yes, it is true that native English words have a charming, earthy quality, but it would be a mistake to extend this idea and suppose that Old English itself was of greater purity, as some people have proposed. That being said, it is still worth recognizing that there is an enormous body of Old English words that would greatly enrich the lexicon of Modern English if they were brought back to life.

Here is a fantastic opportunity: thousands of old, immensely valuable words waiting to be used again. These unique, native words of northern Europe predate the arrival of abstract, refined words from the Mediterranean Basin, and they speak precisely of life in small villages and close-knit societies strongly connected to the land—exactly the kinds of words and values that we so desperately need in modern times. This quest to recover Old English words would be of tremendous value, yet it should be motivated not by a sense that these native English words are somehow "better" but by an awareness that a vast, untapped potential lies at the very heart of the English language.

The following selection of Old English words is derived from Bosworth and Toller's *An Anglo-Saxon Dictionary* (currently being replaced by *The Dictionary of Old English*, a

massive undertaking at the University of Toronto, www.doe.
utoronto.ca).

ac oak

achal oak-whole (=solid)

aefendream evening song

aelf-noth elf-courage

aeppel-tun apple town (=orchard)

afgod an idol

aldor life

anpaeth a solitary path

argebland the sea disturbed by oars

armorgen early morning

belacan to flow around

beogang a swarm of bees

beorsetl beer-settle (=a bench)

beren belonging to a bear

bilehwit bill-white (=the beak of a young bird, i.e., simple or
    sincere)

brytengrund the spacious earth

byrne a stream

clam mud, clay

duce a duck

dunelfen a mountain fairy

eafisc a river fish

eorthling a farmer

feldlic rural

fixen a female fox (=vixen)

flacea snowflakes

foldbold an earthly dwelling

frox frog

gecyn nature

hama cricket

huf a horned owl

lustgrin a snare set by pleasure

lyft air, sky, atmosphere

mearcland a borderland, wilderness

modblind having the mind's eye darkened

os a god or divinity

papolstan a pebble

pinbeam a pine tree

riptima harvest time

rumheort liberal, untroubled

sawelhus soul-house (=the body)

sceadu-genga one who walks in darkness

stancarr rock, stone

tadige toad

untemed wild

uppeland rural countryside

uriglast walking on wet earth

utland a foreign country

welig willow

weorold-mann a man upon earth

widland the face of the earth

widlast a path that stretches far

wille-stream a babbling brook

wilwang a pleasant land

wind-filled blown by the wind

wolcen a cloud

wuduland woodland, forest

wuduwasa a satyr or faun

꙰

Tradition is the "still center" around which innovation orbits.

꙰

DENOTATION

IMAGINE TAKING the Old English word *deor* (a word that gives us Modern English "deer") and tweaking it with a few standard linguistic processes to come up with a word like *doerun* as a noun, verb, or adjective that says something about deer or deer-like behaviors.

The strangeness of a word like *doerun* might scare you away from offering this word to a larger audience, but this would be an unnecessary fear because any word can come to have a clear denotation (meaning) once that word works its way into popular acceptance. In fact, any strange-looking word or string of letters, numbers, or symbols can take on meaning. Think about how readily we all accept and give meaning to formerly meaningless "words" such as *iPod, MP3, Valium,* or *Cheerios,* not to mention emoticons like ;-).

It is a sad commentary that the vast majority of unique new words that enter our vocabulary are corporate slogans designed solely to brand and sell products. Any one of us would hesitate to propose our own new words, yet we eagerly embrace catchy brand names every time a new product comes along.

In experimenting with language you have to remember that the human mind has an astonishing capacity to use and assign meaning to any kind of word or symbol. There is no reason to hold back from putting new words or new meanings on the table—your only task is to be fearless and persuasive.

⚛

If this house were all you ever knew,
would you know the world
or only its spirit?

⚛

ALTERED ORTHOGRAPHY

FROM ITS ORIGINS in Old English and running through most of the Middle Ages, English was governed by few spelling standards. For any given word there could be multiple, even a dozen or more, spellings. In Middle English, for instance, the word *bird* could be spelled *brid, bryd, berd, bred, burd, bord,* or *bridd.*

What was already a confusing situation became even more complicated after the Norman Conquest of 1066, when scribes in charge of copying manuscripts began haphazardly combining Old English and Anglo-Norman spelling systems, doing odd things like replacing *h* with *gh* in words such as *might,* or unsystematically swapping out letters in some groups of words but not in others. By the 1600s it was widely acknowledged that the English spelling system was in shambles.

What happened as spelling reformers gained the upper hand over the next hundred years could only be described as an overcorrection, because it became increasingly common to use new ideas of what constituted "correct or proper spelling" to belittle anyone whose education, social class, or local dialect did not match the new norm. Three hundred years later this attitude is still so deeply entrenched that no one would dare misspell a word today, and spellings have become so rigorously standardized that there is scarcely room for innovation or improvisation. As a consequence, anyone interested in creative language might find it far easier to introduce new words or new word elements than new spellings of already established words.

Ironically, we already accept alternate or variant spellings of some standard English words, and it is clear that the spelling reforms of the 1700s are an ongoing, unfinished process. There are, for example, no single accepted spellings for *color/ colour* or *theater/theatre*, and no verdict on whether to include the silent *e* in *judgement* or *ageing*. Modern English has yet to resolve a host of other nagging questions such as how to spell the past tense forms of verbs like *sauna* (neither *saunaed* nor *sauned* seems to work).

In spite of dictionary-thumping reformers and powerful stigmas against spelling errors, we need to make room for experimenting with the forms (orthography) of words, because this is a source of tremendous creativity and innovation in language. One way to make this process more palatable is to establish up front that the sounds and pronunciation of a word would remain constant if you can easily recognize the original (intended) word. Using the example of *bird*, we might pronounce the word the same way whether it was spelled *byrd, berd, burd,* or *bord*. Such a convention would give a writer some freedom to experiment with creative orthography while still shaping words that can be read and understood when spoken out loud.

The point of playing with orthography is to experiment with new ways of thinking about words. This is not an exercise in spelling words wrong; it is a conscious and highly crafted resculpting of words through sound, form, and historical tradition. If you end up with half a dozen or a dozen variations on *bird* it might create confusion, or it could plant seeds that blossom into new words for another generation of writers. You might even trigger some other important shift; for instance, a version of *bird* in the form *bord* might generate a new and unexpected field of semantic relationships alongside words like *word*, *world*, and *wold*.

Even more intriguing is the possibility that different versions of a word could come to embody slightly different aspects of that object or concept. You could use different versions of *bird* for birds that are migratory versus resident; or for birds in spring, summer, fall, and winter; or for birds that have different symbolic properties. Or, to illustrate with another example, maybe an *aple* could be an unripe apple, an *apple* could be a ripe apple, and an *apel* could be a decaying apple.

§◆

ANGLO-NORMAN

FLIPPING THROUGH the *Anglo-Norman Dictionary* is a fascinating experience. Anglo-Norman is a very old version of French, spoken by Norman invaders who conquered England in 1066, so it seems like an incredibly obscure way to understand Modern English. In fact, Anglo-Norman (also called Anglo-French) has had a profound impact on the English we use today.

What you will find as you browse through the *Anglo-Norman Dictionary* (the seven-volume first edition is being superseded by a second edition, and portions of both are available at www.anglo-norman.net) is a strange mix of words. A large number of words are obviously French, with spellings and sounds that seem totally foreign to English readers, but mixed in with these are an equal number of words that exactly (or almost exactly) match standard words we use today. For instance, in the *Anglo-Norman Dictionary* the word *nonchalance* 'indifferent' (which is a familiar word) immediately precedes the word *nunchalarete* 'indifference' (which looks very odd).

What is going on here is that words that were adapted from Anglo-Norman directly into English at an early date are by now so familiar to us that we recognize them immediately and think of them as "English" words, while words that were never adapted into English look unfamiliar and totally foreign to us. But if English has so readily absorbed thousands of Anglo-Norman words, why couldn't thousands of other equally interesting and useful words be borrowed from Anglo-Norman by modern language-making students?

There is tremendous potential here for a treasure trove of new words to be either adopted straight from Anglo-Norman or else modified to give them a Modern English look and feel. Some of these words would be entirely new to English, while others might mirror words we already use.

Here are some sample words, but I encourage you to explore the *Anglo-Norman Dictionary* and have fun finding your own words to play with.

anubleison cloud

assenti footpath

beleth weasel

bogee badger

chawe a crow

clerseie clear weather

clokke beetle

cocodril crocodile

cupé covered with feathers

cursable running or flowing

danture taming

decressant waning moon

dee swarm of bees

dela beyond the sea

deramer to strip branches from

dragoncel young dragon

ebbé to be stranded by an ebbing tide

ewage water

gaudin of the woods

glatir to howl

gupil fox

hanapel skull

huan owl (also *huhan*)

irounde a swallow (bird)

jargun bird song

mahomerie pagan temple

marage seashore

monosceros unicorn

muke dirt

nuous cloudy

orage wind

perrus rocky

pipee flock of birds

pluvious rainy

ramel of the woods, wild

rivol a stream (also *russel*)

salvagine wild animal

scurel squirrel

sunge dream vision

terrage land

tremble aspen

tuner to thunder

undee torrential rain

upeland the countryside

wibet gnat

~

FRENCH INFLUENCE

AS MENTIONED BEFORE, the Norman conquest of England transformed the English language so dramatically that Modern English bears scant resemblance to its Old English roots. Although the Norman invaders and the conquered peoples of England were both Scandinavian in origin, the Normans ("North Men") were a separate dukedom that had earlier conquered Normandy in northern France and adopted French language and culture, which they carried with them when they later invaded England. As England's new ruling class, Normans flooded Old English with about 37,000 words and word elements derived from French (or from Greek and Latin via their expressions in French).

Many of these new words dealt with objects and ideas that were of interest only to the aristocracy, creating a curiously split society in which English peasants and rural villagers held onto fragments of Old English to refer to the things that mattered to them, while the upper classes spoke of literature, religion, government, law, and chivalry in the elevated register of French. We still recognize vestiges of this low vs. high register (or style) in Modern English. Consider, for example, the fact that we call animals in the barnyard by their "vulgar" Old English names: *cow, calf, pig*, and *sheep*, but we use "refined" French names when we eat them at the dining table: *beef, veal, pork*, and *mutton*. Or think about the subtle levels of refinement expressed when we use the French word *aid* rather than the native word *help*, or *retaliate* instead of *get even*.

One of the most profound impacts of this French invasion was that the heart and soul of Old English—what has been called its *cultural superstructure*—was gutted. Native words for abstract ideas, poetic expressions, and aesthetic nuances were discarded, leaving the dry husk of a language preserved by largely illiterate peasants who continued using the handful of utilitarian words most vital to their lives. When English finally reemerged as a literary language three hundred years later (around the time of Chaucer), an entirely new "superstructure" had to be invented by grafting borrowed words and ideas back onto lingering fragments of the mother tongue.

Although French profoundly influenced the English language and greatly enriched the stock of words and sounds we use today, it is also true that in many cases French words simply replaced native English words that worked just as well. For instance, French gave us important words such as *nature, beast, basin, rock, mountain, island*, and *desert*, but it is worth asking which native words were lost in the process.

Some Aspects of the French Influence

There are many ways that French influenced the language we use today, including changing old Latin words into new forms that are now common in English. For example, French habitually converted the vowels of Latin words into diphthongs, which we now pronounce as single sounds. Thus, Latin *fidem* became French *faith*, and Latin *pictum* became French *paint*. French also had a tendency to co-opt Latin words by clipping them in a distinctive pattern: preserving the first element of the Latin word and stripping away everything else except the stressed syllable. Thus a Latin word like *periculósum* became the French word *perilous*, and the Latin word *rotúndum* became *round*.

Within French itself, there have been major sound changes that are still preserved in Modern English. Thus English has pairs of sounds like the *a* of *rage* from Old French, against the *a* of *mirage* from Late French; similar pairs include the *i* in *vine* vs. *ravine*, the *u* in *duty* vs. *debut*, the *ou* in *count* vs. *tour*, the *ui* in *suit* vs. *suite*, the *g* in *rage* vs. *rouge*, and the *ch* in *chief* vs. *chef*.

The *ch* element shows up in another pairing alongside *c*, with *ch* appearing in words from the Norman French dialect, while *c* was used by other French dialects. This gives us doublets like *chattel* vs. *cattle*, *chant* vs. *cant*, *chariot* vs. *car*, and *chasten* vs. *castigate*.

Another example of old influences that have been preserved is the coexistence of the introduced French sound *gu* alongside the Old English sound *w*, giving us doublets in the pattern of *warranty* vs. *guarantee*, *warden* vs. *guardian*, and *wile* vs. *guile*.

Because French has had a dramatic and well-documented influence on the shape of Modern English, it serves as a model for understanding the ways that languages can change when they come into contact with other languages. It is instructive to realize that in the same way these changes became acceptable over time, they might be legitimately "undone" or taken in other new directions. For instance, why not bring back Old English words that were dropped and replaced by equivalent French words? Old English words like *afgod*, *beorg*, and *blostma* are lovely alternatives to the now-accepted French words *idol*, *mountain*, and *flower*.

§▲

Pray save me from mod-blind madness
where "mod" is not mad but mind inside man.

§▲

THE MYSTERY OF MEN-

FEW ASPECTS OF HUMAN experience have so mystified people across all time as the inexplicable workings of our own minds. We now comfortably assign every activity of our minds to our heads, specifically to our brains, but ancient Greeks believed that all forms of thinking and feeling originated in the center of the chest. It is, in fact, a fascinating exercise to let go of your self-conscious "headedness" and practice shifting your perceptions of thinking and feeling to the center of your chest.

The active forces of the mind—including thinking, perceiving, and remembering—are linguistically captured in the

Indo-European root *men-* (found in words like *mantra* and *mental*). And while we now think of these cognitive activities as mere abstractions flickering passively in some imaginary mental space, this is misleading because it makes us forget that mental activity is in fact strongly linked to physical action and to the physical world (as when we say "I shudder at the thought" or "my thoughts go out to you").

This then is a call to take your "mind" outside—into the natural world and out of your head—in search of the contours and experiences of mind in the physical world. Examine, experience, and feel the details of the earth around you. What type of mind is present in the blowing of the wind, the dancing of leaves, the passage of seasons? How might a mind be expressing itself to you at this very moment? Are there aspects of this mind waiting to be named or described?

In Middle English they spoke of the mind as *mund* or *mend*, and we are at once reminded of the Spanish word *mundo* ('the world'), as well as the threads that stitch the world together. Step outside and experience this web of *mind, world,* and *threads* weaving together in the language you create.

꧁꧂

Our current knowledge is all "cutting edge."
This is all that seems to matter: edge, edge, edge.
But there is no interior habitat of the mind in this picture.

"Only in words does mind speak its own language. Only in the creative word is [the mind] in its perfect freedom...."
—Ernest Robert Curtius, *European Literature and the Latin Middle Ages*

꧁꧂

PRAYER AND BLESSING
FORMULA

PRAYER AND BLESSING FORMULA are ways of using language to express our relationships with the deeper mysteries of life, and our ever-evolving understanding of these relationships is encoded in the shapes, sounds, and structures of sacred language. So vital is this task that "wordsmiths" in ancient cultures (those who we call "poets" today) were highly valued as praise-makers and prophets. They were believed to possess divine knowledge because the language of their highly crafted phrases differed so dramatically from common speech.

The importance of putting words together with great skill and intention is evidenced by the many examples of ancient writings that begin with invocations such as "I weave these words" or "I offer these words"—and it is this elevated and carefully crafted language that merits our attention. In modern times, it has become habitual for us to speak *about* things as if they were nothing more than inert objects, but the power of prayer and blessing formula is that they ask us to turn this around and speak *to* things, because all things merit attention and compassion.

The language of the world's sacred literature is beautiful and haunting, and a large part of what we pick up on is this careful crafting of words. Even the set phrases and themes of blessing formula have a special potency because they are repeated time after time, and are handed down between generations. If you can imagine how important grains and wine would have been to an ancient agricultural society, you might begin to grasp the power of repeated blessing formulas like "May Ceres give grain" or "May Liber give wine" (Ceres and Liber were regenerative nature deities whose names are now found in our words *cereal* and *libation*).

The poet's craft included creating not only beautiful expressions but also messages hidden in the text that wove in added layers of divine meaning. One elegant example can be found in the opening stanza of Sappho's hymn to Aphrodite, the goddess of love. The first word of the hymn is *poikilothron* and the closing words are *potnia thumon*, and hidden in both are the letters of the Greek word *pothon* 'desire' (details in Watkins, *How to Kill a Dragon*). It is as if a modern writer wrote "glad we stir with life, maddened by siren calls" as a way to hide the word *desire*.

Repetition and hidden messages are but two examples of the many tools and techniques used to shape words in sacred literature, and I encourage you to find other examples. In this language-making task there is no endpoint; there is simply the steady, lifelong practice of speaking to the world through prayers and blessings. If even a small part of this attentiveness shows up in your writing, then we will all be moved one step closer to a deeper and healthier relationship with the world around us.

Christians co-opted the Old Dutch word heilig
*('the charisma surrounding a pagan king')
and turned it into our modern word* healing.

GENIUS LOCI

ONE OF THE MOST fascinating aspects of ancient Greek and Roman cultures is the way they populated the land and their homes with a great number of particularized deities. Every family had its own household gods and goddesses; every field, wood, spring, cave, or other notable natural feature had its own guardian spirits; and even individual trees or rocks might be the homes of highly localized deities of one kind or another. Minor deities also looked after things as specific as the first leaves of the crops or the first cries of a newborn baby.

Such a diverse pantheon reflects a highly refined engagement with the texture of life in a particular landscape, so it is instructive to look at the kinds of deities that were once celebrated. These named deities might not have any bearing on our modern world, but they can still inspire us to think of new ways to repopulate the world with divine spirits. There is, after all, a profound psychic, emotional, and aesthetic appeal in recognizing and naming nodes of vital energy around us.

We need to reanimate our world: to recognize, honor, and celebrate the unique presences that coalesce at specific points in the landscape or at specific points in our lives. The severing of this bond, and the doubt that this disconnection creates, is what opens up space for corporations to step in and harvest people and resources without protest. We need to protect each other as well as the land, and we need the help of allies we don't speak to anymore.

Here is a brief selection of words from the divine literature of Greece and Rome:

aedes the dwelling place of a god or goddess, typically a temple or shrine

dryads nymphs of forests and oaks

fanum a sacred space or sanctuary

feriae a festival in celebration of a deity

genius loci the presiding spirit of a place

ianus an entrance to a sacred spot; also the god of entrances (=Janus)

lararium a shrine for the *lares* (household deities)

lucus any sacred grove or wood (also *nemus*)

naiads nymphs associated with the gentle motion of water in springs, rivers, and fountains

numen any divine or supernatural power

nymphs feminine deities associated with natural objects or places (called "children of the earth" by Hesiod)

oreads nymphs of mountains and grottoes

satyrs woodland spirits who represented the vital powers of nature

sibyls prophetesses who lived around remote caves or springs

The actual names of gods and goddesses were usually considered taboo and kept secret. Deities would instead be addressed with alternate names or with vague formulaic phrases such as "the one whose name is forever blessed." The reason for this is that names convey power and could be misused if someone stole the name (much like what happens when developers tear up beautiful places and then name their developments after the sites they have desecrated). Scholars have therefore had a hard time uncovering the real names of the hundreds of gods and goddesses celebrated in Greek and Roman times, but here are a few names that have come down to us.

Abnoba a goddess of hunting and forests

Aether a personification of the upper sky or clear bright air

Clivicola a goddess who guarded slopes

Collatina a goddess of the hills

Dea Dia a goddess of planted seeds and new crops

Feronia a goddess of orchards, groves, and woods

Fulgora a goddess of lightning

Maia a goddess of growing things (=the month of May)

Mens a goddess of the mind or thoughts

Nerthus an earth goddess

Penates spirits of the hearth and household

Psyche the personification of the human soul

Silvanus a god of woods and fields

Terminus a god of boundary stones and landmarks

Terra the goddess of the earth

Vallonia the goddess of valleys

Virbius a forest god

Again, it is worth considering these lists of divine names and deities, not because we are going to start using these names but because they demonstrate a nuanced and refined sense of sacredness that has been largely lost in modern times. Think of these lists as an invitation to recognize and honor places and events that have special significance in your life. This is an opportunity for language-making, a chance to create new names that are full of meaning; whether the names are shared with public audiences, or highly personal and never divulged to anyone else.

It has been noted that in all the poetry of antiquity nature was always presented as inhabited, and it didn't matter whether it was inhabited by humans or gods.

Greek limodoron *'gift of the water meadow.'*

GREEK INFLUENCE

GREEK MAY BE THIRD on the list of the top three foreign languages that have contributed words to English, but it still has an outsized impact because it profoundly influenced the first and second languages on the list (Latin and French). Romans borrowed many Greek words and grammar rules as they shaped Latin, and many of these same elements then morphed into French as it developed out of Latin. As a consequence, Modern English may have relatively few words or rules derived directly from Greek, but many Greek words and rules still made it into English through the filters of Latin and French.

The contributions of Greek to English can be divided into three groups: words that entered English through Latin (and French), words that were copied directly from ancient Greek writers during periods of enthusiasm for classical literature, and modern words that have been formed using Greek affixes and combining forms.

Old English was a Germanic language that had little connection with Greek language or culture, but a handful of Greek words were still introduced into Old English as Christianity began to spread throughout Europe. Early loanwords from Greek included *church, bishop, devil, priest,* and *monk.* But after this brief initial infusion, Greek dropped out of the picture until direct borrowing started up again with a revival of interest in classical culture in 1540 (after a gap of nearly a thousand years).

However, Greek's most significant contributions began after the 1800s, when it became a significant and highly productive source of technical words in the scientific and medical fields. Rather than contributing words, however, Greek now contributes "combining forms" (elements of old words that are used as building blocks for new words). For example, *bio* is a combining form that gives us new words like *biology* and *biotech,* while *eco* gives us words like *ecology* and *eco-friendly.*

Along with combining forms, Greek has also given English some highly productive prefixes and suffixes. These piggy-backed into English on borrowed words, but were then separated from their host words and freely added to other words to create new "English" words. Examples include *-ize,* which has become the most productive Greek suffix in Modern English.

A few common Greek affixes and combining forms are listed below, but you should consult a specialized dictionary for a complete list. My favorite dictionaries for this purpose are Jaeger's *Sourcebook of Biological Names and Terms* and Borror's *Dictionary of Word Roots and Combining Forms.* I encourage you to spend a lot of time with these dictionaries because they provide the raw material for a lifetime of new word formation.

- Notice that affixes and combining forms often start out as freestanding nouns, adjectives, or prepositions and only later become dependent affixes through long association with other words. Elements that started as Greek nouns include *anthropo-, bio-, cephalo-, helio-, litho-, logo-,* and *physio-*. Elements that started as Greek adjectives include *acro-*, *aero-*, *hemi-*, *macro-*, *micro-*, *neo-*, and *poly-*. And elements that started as Greek prepositions include *anti-*, *apo-*, *hyper-*, *meta-*, *peri-*, and *syn-*. This is instructive because it shows how you could invent new affixes and combining forms from a wide variety of words.

- Notice also that affixes and combining forms are usually placed at the beginning of words (as prefixes or word-initial elements) or at the end of words (as suffixes or word-final elements), but you could experiment with putting them in the middle of words (as infixes).

a- not, without

anti- against, opposite

apo- away from

dia- through, across

epi- on, near

hyper- over, beyond

meta- next to, changed

peri- around

pro- in front of

syn- together with

-asm converts verbs into nouns denoting the result of a condition

-ess forms nouns denoting a female agent

-ism creates nouns signifying an action, belief, or condition

-ist creates nouns denoting an agent or doer of an action

-ize creates verbs (mostly from adjectives) signifying an activity related to the root word

-*ma* forms abstract nouns that are the result of an action or condition

-*oid* forms nouns for something resembling a shape or form

-*on* (plural -*a*) forms nouns denoting a basic unit

-*sis* forms abstract nouns signifying an action or result

Creating new words by adding Greek affixes (or combining forms) to root words may be the only easy way to tap into the immense wealth of the Greek tradition. Sadly, due to the tremendous difficulty of reading ancient Greek, it is not likely that many people will turn to original Greek sources in search of old words to pull forward, but for anyone who has a working knowledge of Greek or wants to take on this challenge, there is a wealth of words waiting to be carried over into English. For the rest of us, it might be instructive to trace the paths of a few English words that have originated from Greek sources so we can peek at some of the fascinating ways that this language-making process has worked in the past.

The Greek word *ereipein* 'to tear down' seems to have led to the Latin word *ripa* 'bank of a river,' then to the later (Vulgar) Latin word *riparia* 'river.' The form of the word changed into Anglo-Norman and Middle English *rivere*, then dropped the silent *e* in Modern English *river*.

The Greek word *Okeanos* 'a great river circling the earth' became the Latin word *oceanus*, then Anglo-Norman and Middle English *occean* and finally Modern English *ocean*.

The Greek word *era* 'earth' is connected with the Old German word *ero*, then Old English *eorthe*, followed by Middle English *erthe* and finally Modern English *earth*.

The Greek word *lakkos* 'a pond' became the Latin word *lacus*, then Anglo-Norman and Middle English *lac* and finally Modern English *lake*.

The Greek word *phasianos* 'pheasant' became the Latin word *phasianus*, then Anglo-Norman *faisan*, followed by Middle English *fesant* and finally Modern English *pheasant*.

The Greek word *mys* 'mouse' became the Latin word *mūs*, then Old German and Old English *mūs*, followed by Middle English *mous* and finally Modern English *mouse*.

The Greek word *pitys* 'pine' seems to have led to the Latin word *pinus*, then Old English *pīn*, followed by Middle and Modern English *pine*.

"[The Presocratics of Ancient Greece] were devoted to the primary task of inventing a language which would make future systems possible.
—Eric Havelock,
Preface to Plato

LATIN INFLUENCE

ENGLISH HAS HAD A LONG, complex, and fascinating relationship with Latin. Many traces of this rich legacy permeate every aspect of the language we use today, and this deep influence continues at a faster rate than at any point in history due to the prevalence of Latin affixes and roots in the formation of modern scientific terminology.

It is astounding that an ancient "dead" language has had such a lasting impact on English. Not only was Latin a richly expressed classical language, but it is a testament to its versatility that throughout the tumultuous and fractured Middle Ages it endured and even deepened its range of expressive power by morphing into the default language of the Church and all higher learning. Even in the darkest times, when much of the population of Europe struggled just to survive each day, a handful of scholars and theologians kept Latin and the flame of knowledge alive in small, isolated enclaves.

Latin's influence on English began at a very early date as Roman military campaigns and merchants spread their tentacles far and wide throughout Western Europe. For instance, the Roman general Julius Caesar invaded Britain in 55 BC, beginning an occupation that was to last nearly four hundred years. Early Germanic peoples did not have much use for Latin but still absorbed a variety of words used by merchants or by government and Church institutions. The Anglo-Saxons eventually borrowed six hundred to seven hundred words from Latin (compared to 51,000 Latin words in Modern English), including basic cooking and food words such as *wine, kitchen, fork, cheese, cook, cup, butter,* and *kettle.*

Latin loanwords continued to flow into English due to several influential factors, including the Church and the fact that important thinkers were endlessly fascinated by the classical tradition; there was also a massive influx of Latin words into English via the Romance languages (especially French). Many aspects of English—from the "Roman" alphabet, to the sounds of our letters, to the forms of many words—were eventually derived from or shaped by Latin. Ultimately, Latin has added more words to the English lexicon than any other language, and perhaps even more importantly it has contributed an extensive list of elements that have been phenomenally productive in the creation of new English words.

Latin words have often been borrowed in their original, intact forms, but it is far more common for the roots to be preserved while the endings are dropped or replaced with a silent *e* to make the words more closely resemble native English words. For example, the Latin word *fragilis* gave us our Modern English word *fragile*. Due to the Norman Conquest and a long history of exchanges between English and French-speaking peoples, Latin words have also been adopted along with their French endings (e.g., *gener-ous, prefer-ence, glori-fy*).

The desire to revive and imitate Latin traditions has also led to many idiosyncratic results, especially during the Renaissance of the 1500s, when classical enthusiasts artificially inserted letters into words to make them look more "Latin" (i.e., more scholarly or more learned). These self-conscious efforts resulted in a large number of English words with oddly placed letters (originally all silent but increasingly pronounced to varying degrees) in words like *debt, doubt, subtle, verdict, adventure, author, fault,* and *receipt*. At its worst, this resurgence of interest in all things classical led to the creation of unconventional imitation words that raised the hackles of an old guard who scornfully dismissed these overblown Latinisms as "inkhorn terms." Some of these invented words were truly awful (e.g., *illecebrous, deruncinate, suppeditate*), but quite a few innovative inkhorn terms from the Renaissance endured and became part of Modern English (e.g., *decorum, intersperse, hiatus*).

By far, the most pervasive and productive influence of Latin lies in the many affixes and combining elements (also called combining forms or bound roots) introduced to the English language (see Miller's *Latin Suffixal Derivatives in English* for a comprehensive, though rather technical, introduction to Latin suffixes). For the language-making student this is where things get juicy. Not only do these affixes and combining elements offer countless ways to create new words, they can also alter the fundamental ways that words are used. For instance, the suffix -*ary* turns the verb *imagine* into the adjective *imaginary*, while -*ate* turns the noun *anima* into the verb *animate*, and in the same way you can use this process to transform almost any word into something new.

Latin affixes are covered elsewhere in this book so I will not describe them here, and combining elements are best covered in specialized dictionaries (I recommend Jaeger's *Sourcebook of Biological Names and Terms* or Borror's *Dictionary of Word Roots and Combining Forms*), but there are several other aspects of the Latin influence that need to be mentioned.

First of all, there is a lot of overlap between Greek and Latin borrowings (plus Greek and Latin elements can be combined to create hybrid words), but in general Greek elements are restricted to specialized words (e.g., *anesthesia*) while Latin elements give us familiar words (e.g., *famous*). English can even borrow roots with the same meaning from both Greek and Latin and then use them for different purposes in accordance with this rule. Thus, two roots meaning 'to creep'—*herp* in Greek and *serp* in Latin—give us the specialized word *herptile* alongside the generalized word *serpent*.

It is also helpful to remember that Latin words have often been borrowed and reborrowed multiple times, raising the possibility that each time they have an opportunity to create a new form of the same core word. An example of the same word being borrowed three times is the Latin *regalis*, which came into English directly as *regal* (notice that the ending is dropped), then entered again through French (via Chaucer) to give us *real*, and then again at a later time as *royal*. An example of a word being borrowed four times is the Latin *discus*, which turns up in Old English as *dish* and then in Middle English as *desk*, but then is borrowed from French as *dais* and from Latin again as *disc*.

Finally, it is worth making the important point that there

are many rules governing the ways we can make new words from Latin (and Greek) elements (for a concise summary of some important rules, see Denning et. al. *English Vocabulary Elements*, chapter 6). These rules are vital to the extent that they govern the many ways that letters and sounds have traditionally been altered to facilitate the awkward transition from one language to another. At the same time these rules are cumbersome and complex, with names like *phonation assimilation, cluster simplification*, and *final stop deletion*. But, like all rules, they are conventions designed to create something that people expect to see (in this case "properly" formed words).

Each language-making student will have to decide whether to learn and follow these rules or push language into new terrain by experimenting with exotic forms that may or may not be rejected because the rules are not being followed. There is no right answer, and either choice would be an equally valid and exciting path to take.

> *"new wine in new skin"*
> —Stefan George,
>   nineteenth-century
>   German poet

> *not every word needs an etymology*
> —an idea from Isidore of
>   Seville, seventh-century
>   Spanish bishop (considered
>   the last scholar of the
>   ancient world)

TIPS FOR RECOGNIZING GREEK AND LATIN WORDS

THE PROCESS OF BRINGING old elements together to form new words has traditionally been ruled by a convention that Greek elements should be combined with other Greek elements and Latin elements with Latin elements. Either because few people are familiar with classical languages or for the sake of novelty, this convention has been frequently broken with unexpected hybrid combinations, but the guideline is still a useful tool.

However, unless you consult a specialized dictionary, it is hard to have an intuitive understanding for what differentiates Greek and Latin elements, so here are a few tips to assist you in recognizing letters or letter combinations that signal one language or the other. These tips (adapted from Denning et. al. *English Vocabulary Elements*) are not ironclad, due to exceptions, but they are still helpful starting points.

Suspect that an element might be Greek if it contains:

- The letter *k* at the beginning. Examples include *kaleido-, kera-, kilo-, kyrio-*.

- The letter *y*. Examples include *crypto-, cyan-, dy-, gyn-, hygr-, hyper-, oxy-, poly-, -sophy, thym-*.

- The letter *z*. Examples include *-ize, oz-, pez-, soz-, syzg-, trapez-, zabr-, zirco-, zon-, zoo-, zym-*.

- Combinations of letters in the form *ch, ph, rh*, or *th*. Examples include *charact-, chrom-, -phobia, troph-, rhamph-, rhin-, path-, theo-*.

- Unusual letters or pairs of consonants at the beginning of an element: *mn, pn, ps, pt, and x.* Examples include *mnem-, mnest-, pneum-, pnig-, psitt-, psych-, pter-, ptil-, xanth-, xyl-.*

  (Note that the letter *o* is often inserted when forming new words from Greek elements: *kaleid-o-scope, macr-o-cosm, micr-o-scope, psych-o-logy, rhin-o-ceros, rhod-o-dendron, therm-o-meter.*)

Latin elements are less distinctive, but suspect a Latin source if an element contains letters that are absent in Greek:

- The letter *f.* Examples include *fer-, for-, fund-.*

- The letter *j.* Examples include *jub-, jug-, juv-.*

- The letter combination *qu.* Examples include *quadr-, qual-, quasi-.*

- The letter *v.* Examples include *valv-, vari-, vert-.*

  (Note that the letter *i* may be inserted when forming new words from Latin elements: *aud-i-tory, carn-i-vorous, cune-i-form, fluv-i-al, ped-i-cure, strat-i-graphy, verm-i-form, vin-i-culture.*)

❧

*"Learning in symbolic form that the past can be mastered
is as important as learning in dramatic form
that your choices resonate."*
—Adam Gopnik

❧

MEDIEVAL LATIN

*"The isolation of medieval Latin from everyday usage
proved to be a significant advantage [because] the freedom
of words from current associations…made it relatively
easy… to create a clear and precise language."*
—Erich Auerbach, *Literary
Language and Its Public in
Late Latin Antiquity and
in the Middle Ages*

AT FIRST GLANCE there are no obvious reasons why anyone should spend time studying Medieval Latin. Even though Latin has had a massive influence on English, it is still an obscure topic for most people, and Medieval Latin barely registers at all.

So what is Medieval Latin and why does it matter? If you think about Latin as a language or as a literature, you are almost certainly thinking about Classical Latin, the highly refined, high-status form of Latin that was the language of literature and poetry during the great flowering of Roman culture (roughly 100 BC to AD 100). The shape and grammar of Classical Latin was first honed and polished by brilliant writers such as Cicero, Ovid, and Virgil, then frozen in place and passed down from generation to generation through countless teachers and grammar books.

But the Roman Empire eventually grew too large and bloated to withstand the increasing invasions of barbarian tribes, and the Empire collapsed around AD 400. In the absence of a central authority Europe descended into the chaos of the Dark Ages, and knowledge of Classical Latin (or any kind of higher learning, for that matter) was nearly lost except at a few scattered outposts of the Church. Then, after centuries of darkness, there was a revival of Latin (*renovatio*) during the Carolingian Renaissance of the late 700s, when King Charlemagne recruited a scholar by the name of Alciun to patch together a reconstituted form of Latin that we now call Medieval Latin.

It is important to realize that Latin never really died out. It is true that the Classical Latin of the educated elite disappeared with the demise of the Roman Empire, but there had always been an unwritten Vulgar Latin spoken by the vast majority of the (mostly uneducated) Roman population. This spoken Vulgar Latin did not fade with the end of the Empire; it simply merged with the languages of invading tribes and morphed into local vernacular languages that became the building blocks of Spanish, French, Italian, and other Romance languages.

When King Charlemagne was designated as the first Holy Roman Emperor in AD 800, he became responsible for managing a huge swath of central Europe. It was almost impossible to rule an empire divided by competing local languages, so Charlemagne needed one unifying language, and Alciun was the right person for the formidable task of developing this language. Hailed as the most learned man of his time, Alciun was a native of Britain, which had the remarkable distinction of being an isolated outpost of the Roman Empire that had managed to keep classical knowledge alive even after the breakup of the Empire. Alciun was a brilliant man, but he was also the product of an insular society far removed from the epicenter of Roman culture. As a consequence, when Charlemagne invited Alciun to his court for the purpose of creating a unifying language (which by default had to be Latin), Alciun assumed he was using Classical Latin as his model when in fact he was working with the Latin he knew best, an idiosyncratic "British" Latin that had taken shape over several hundred years at a remote outpost surrounded by Anglo-Saxon (English-speaking) peoples.

It goes without saying that the result was uneven. But even if Alciun had created a perfectly realized language or a perfectly restored form of Classical Latin, the hard truth was that the writers, scholars, and administrators of Charlemagne's vast empire were largely untrained and unschooled. Furthermore, their first languages were local vernacular languages, and in every case Latin was no more than an imperfectly understood second language.

However, this is exactly the point where Medieval Latin gets really interesting. It not only gives us a model for how an entire language can be molded from the structure of another major language more or less within a single generation; it also shows us that a derived language can be incredibly dynamic and alive. Right from the start, writers began modifying Medieval Latin with all kinds of quirky solutions; if they did not understand which Latin word to use or how to construct a sentence in Latin, they simply made something up or borrowed conventions from their first language. As a result, Medieval Latin became a hybrid language with many fascinating, quickly changing, and loosely interpreted word shapes, sounds, and rules (for example, the word *maeremium* 'timber,' ended up with over fifty different spellings).

As the *de facto* literary language of its time, this strangely flexible form of Latin was also self-consciously put to the task of describing the new technologies, inventions, concepts, and values that were rapidly becoming part of life in the Middle Ages. This is why Medieval Latin is such a valuable model for the language-making student—it shows us how readily a language broken from its restrictive past can be used in the service of new ideas.

Sadly, not many people will ever tap into the treasures of Medieval Latin, and few libraries or individuals in the world have the resources to purchase the seventeen-volume *Dictionary of Medieval Latin Based on British Sources*, published by Oxford University Press (though it is currently being digitized and will hopefully become more accessible in the future). Fortunately, the *Revised Medieval Latin Word-List* by R. E. Latham is available for a reasonable price, and this relatively compact dictionary can still introduce readers to a basic vocabulary.

Here then are some words from Latham's dictionary to give you a taste of Medieval Latin. It is telling that many of these words are Latin in form but have been derived from vernacular sources or else modified from Classical Latin through different filters. Medieval Latin is an intriguing language exactly because it is this strange and somewhat haunting mix of words and solutions.

adsisa the sound of waves coming ashore

astrifugus putting the stars to flight

babillo someone who babbles

batrax a toad

cohos the total content of the human body

cormiranda a cormorant

covata a group of swans

damus deer

diaconios a waxing moon

dionysia a sunflower

divortium an out-of-the-way place

effulminatus struck by lightning

evolatio bird flight

falcula a swallow (bird)

gleba a field

gronna a marsh or marshy spot

hinnibile the neighing of a horse

hokum a strip of meadow

indigator a tracker

infolio to wrap or fold up in petals

isculus an earthworm

lacualis living in lakes

laya a path through the woods

muriceps a mouse-catcher, cat

nomannia no-man's-land

porpasius a porpoise

portunus an elf

scropes rocks

scytala a weasel

spissum a thicket of brambles or bushes

tonitrum the ringing of thunder

turdula a little thrush

utlanda the "outland," wilderness

zinzito to chirp

zoticus life-giving

The entire history of Latin words in Britain from AD *800 to 1800 included countless words that were dead-ends, that were used only once, or that were invented, Latinized forms of highly local words used by farmers and peasants. But out of this mix rose a richly evolving language.*

YE OLDE WORDES

WHAT IS IT that distinguishes words like *damsel, henceforth, smitten, thee, 'twas,* or *yuletide*? These words are archaisms—borrowings from an earlier stage of the language—and whether it is the words themselves or the ways the words are used, archaisms imply quaint or old-fashioned values. They show up in nursery rhymes and fairy tales, and are often used to create special effects (as in a business name like *Ye Olde Bookshoppe*), giving the popular impression that archaisms are outdated and childish.

But surprisingly, one of the most influential books in the English language relies heavily on archaisms to great effect. The King James Bible was consciously constructed from archaisms to give this important book its characteristically dignified and powerful voice. The committees of writers who shaped the King James opted for countless archaisms such as "follow thou me" or "they knew him not," even when contemporary alternatives made more sense. Other examples of the powerful use of archaisms can be found in two important poems, Edmund Spenser's *Faerie Queen* and John Milton's *Paradise Lost.*

It is a mistake to dismiss archaisms. They speak of tradition and roots, and can reconnect us with bedrock values that modern society sorely lacks. Old words brought to life again can be the chief building blocks, the cornerstones, of a well-laid foundation, and they deserve your careful attention.

❧

BRING FORWARD OLD WORDS IN NEW WAYS

❧

NEWFOUNDLAND ENGLISH

IF THERE IS A GOLD MINE hidden in the English language, it might be the scarcely known variant of English spoken on the Canadian island of Newfoundland. Systematically documented for the first time in the 1982 *Dictionary of Newfoundland English*, there is probably no other form of modern living English with such a rich and well-developed vocabulary for speaking of nature and the rustic rural life.

This is the English of a hardscrabble people who have been living on the land and from the sea in their own isolated corner of the world for over four hundred years. In the face of a notoriously frugal and uncertain way of life, Newfoundlanders have turned to their language as an exuberant counterbalance, and the result is nothing short of spectacular—a brilliantly expressive and playful lexicon that recognizes and celebrates nearly every aspect of the natural world and the simple rural lifestyle.

Newfoundland English is a language that immediately immerses you in a world of snow, ocean waves, storms, hunting cabins, trap lines, native berries, fish, seals, and seasonal festivals. Ice conditions are described as *ballicatter, quarr, sish,* and *slob*; the sea is a *blue drop*; a seal is a *bedlamer* or a *jar*; a grebe is a *spraw-foot*; a dolphin a *squid hound.*

The charm of Newfoundland English is twofold: it preserves a centuries-old dialect from the English countryside that has largely died out elsewhere, and it folds into this old matrix a dynamic, living tapestry of words that reflect a people's deep and highly personal engagement with their remote landscape. Newfoundland English is a model and inspiration to anyone looking for ways that English might speak more eloquently of the natural world.

Here are a few sample words that convey the spirit of Newfoundland English:

aspy thick with aspen trees

bawn meadow

biff junco

bobby-rooter fox sparrow

brew a verb for the behavior of playing seals

champkin participant in a mummer's play

conkerbill icicle

drash heavy rain

duckish twilight, dusk

dung mixen snow

garnipper large mosquito

middler a beaver between its second and third year

naked man cairn of rocks

nip a difficult spot on a path

pant the swelling of ocean waves

queak the gentle squeak of a small animal
roaration a deep and prolonged noise
snarbuckle a burnt piece of food
stog to fill the chinks in a log cabin with moss
tished water barely frozen with a thin layer of ice
wind light a gleam of light moving over the ocean surface

❧

"Every language is an old-growth forest of the mind."
—Wade Davis

❧

NEW BE-KENNINGS

KENNINGS ARE A FORM of skillful wordplay best known from Old Norse and Old English poems but which run as a thread through many languages of the Indo-European tradition. In their most basic form, kennings are created by substituting a two-word phrase for a noun. What elevates the kenning into the realm of play, imagination, and ritual is that the replacement nouns do not name the thing directly, so the link must be discovered.

Kennings are in essence miniature riddles (consider the strange logic of modern "kennings" like *airhead, couch potato, sound-bite,* or *spin doctor*), but it would be a mistake to dismiss them as trivial wordplay. They are, in fact, powerful teaching tools that ask the reader (or listener) to access the imaginative and intellectual resources of their culture in search of meaning. This vital function is implied by the verb *kenna*, which has been variously translated as 'to make known (by)' or 'to describe, recognize, teach' (the Old Norse word *kenningar* also means 'symbols'). In traditional cultures, kennings helped preserve the formulas and rituals of the past by keeping them current and active in the formation of new "riddles." Thus, the very complex Old Norse kenning "stave of the icicle of the tumult of axes," which stood as a substitute for the word *warrior*, could be meaningful only so long as the audience recalled the images and legends of their past.

Kennings closely resemble compounds in which words (usually nouns, but also nouns and other words) are put together to form new words, but they differ from compounds because the elements are usually framed in a genitive relationship. In other words, the elements of a kenning are made dependent on each other in the same way we use *of* or modify a word with the possessive *'s* in Modern English (e.g., "the home of deer" or "the deer's home").

Compound words are common in Modern English and include words like *dragonfly, sunflower,* and *riverbank*; and they were abundant in Old Norse and Old English, with examples ranging from *laughter-smith* ('a minstrel') and *go-weaver* ('spider') to *wolf-head-tree* ('a gallows'). Kennings were also very common, and in some old manuscripts nearly every noun is either a kenning or a compound. Common kennings include the many Old English kennings for "sea" such as *whale's road, cup of waves, gannet's bath*, or *bridle-path of the sail*. Other evocative examples of compounds and kennings include *bone-house* ('body'), *leaving of waves* ('sand'), *heath-stepper* ('stag'), and *peace-weaver* ('woman').

The mere arrangement of words was one thing, but the highly valued "compression of meaning" that seamlessly wove together tradition and innovation took a lifetime of devoted scholarship to master. For example, the beguilingly simple kenning *one-paths* outwardly described a path so narrow that only one person at a time could walk it, but for members of a warrior society it symbolized the ultimate terror—a place where you could not walk side by side with your companions or where the tribe could not come to your rescue—and you can almost feel the dread falling on warriors as they sat around a campfire listening to this tale.

Because compounds and kennings were so abundant in Old Norse and Old English literature, great value was placed on a writer's originality and skill. The challenges of creating innovative new kennings within a rigidly constrained traditional framework pushed these writers to the highest perfection of this form, and only the most accomplished masters secured wealth, fame, and royal patronage.

In light of these deep traditions it is both inspiring and a little intimidating to try to create meaningful kennings in Modern English. Fortunately, one of the pleasures and benefits of kennings is that they ask you to think about the enduring threads and underlying values of your culture, because these are the things that must be skillfully condensed in a finely crafted kenning. Even without this depth it is still fun to craft these little word riddles and see how far you can take them. Try experimenting with various combinations of nouns, verbs, adjectives, adverbs, and prepositions, and consider what it might mean to say things like *bee-sky, branch-above, earth-bride,* or *brim-wolf.*

❧

Where is the language-generating energy of our time?

❧

FOX TURNS

AS A NATURALIST, I was delighted to discover that Old Norse poets used the term *fox turn* to describe one of the figures of speech they relied on to create highly refined poetic verses. In this case, *fox turn* refers to the dodging and darting behavior of a running fox as metaphorically applied to verses in which successive units play with unexpected contrast.

Our modern term for this same figure of speech is *antithesis*, a term rather dryly derived from classical rhetoric, but what is remarkable about Old Norse poetry is that many of their poetic terms were drawn from vivid images of the natural world. As another example, Norse poets referred to the technique of dropping a syllable to shorten a poetic line (what we call *catalexis*) with the same word that meant 'to dock an animal's tail.'

What is beautiful about Old Norse terminology is that it asked both writers and readers to pay attention to the natural world because the vocabulary of poetic and stylistic expression drew heavily from powerful images and patterns found in nature. We currently describe figures of speech with classical Greek terms that have a lofty, educated air about them, but what if we instead invented new terms that were grounded in the earth and connected to a life spent observing plants, animals, land, and water? This may seem silly, but doesn't it make sense that something vital shifts when a culture describes its poetic and literary language with an eye toward the natural world?

☙

Why are there so few nature-specific verbs in the English language?

☙

NATURE RHETORIC

RHETORIC IS A VERY COMPLEX subject that has deeply occupied philosophers and thinkers since Plato introduced the term around 385 BC. In ancient times, rhetoric was hailed as one of the central pillars of democratic discourse and clear thinking, but in modern times rhetoric has been more readily dismissed as mere "style" or criticized for the ways it can be used to manipulate an argument for a speaker's benefit.

In brief, rhetoric is simply the arrangement of words and ideas into patterns that best convey your intentions to an audience. The poet Jane Hirshfield eloquently described rhetoric as "the precise and beautiful movement of mind in language." Traditionally, the highest aim of rhetoric was to teach, delight, and inspire an audience by instructing its practitioners in the subtle arts of invention, arrangement, style, memory, and delivery.

Rhetoric is therefore a crafting, and its product is a vessel that holds thought and wisdom. As it is usually taught, this crafting utilizes abstract patterns generated in the mind, but why not construct rhetoric from the patterns of nature?

For instance, if you think of your text as a trail, do you walk it slowly, absorbing every detail along the way, or do you walk it quickly so you feel the shape of the land? What happens if you run the trail or backpack it? Could you trace the landscape like a bird or a mountain lion or a worm? Do you follow the edges of patterns or cut across them?

Once you begin thinking about patterns in nature you soon realize that any one of them could serve as a template to shape and inform your rhetoric. How about a lightning strike: the way it builds up electricity in a rising thunderstorm, flashes with intense light, pauses, and then rolls with thunder? Or the way that the seasons divide the year into parts, each with its own energy? Or the way tadpoles and caterpillars graze and grow slowly, pause, and then metamorphose into gorgeous adult animals? Or the way photosynthesis works in a predetermined chemical dance (a kind of meter) to create glowing greens, nourishing sugars, and complicated food chains? Or how about the patterns in a flower: the central stem, the arrangement of petals in a circle, the holding of nectar, the release of seeds?

Patterns "out there" in nature give us an instruction manual of what is shapely and beautiful, so why not use these designs as the basis for your own personal rhetoric? Even if the patterns do not immediately rise to the surface in your writing, they still offer a way to apprentice yourself and model your mind after nature—a way to continue standing side by side with the natural world even when you are working at your desk.

There is no right way to do this; simply hold these patterns in your mind as you craft your compositions—word by word, sentence by sentence, idea by idea—and observe how these patterns shape the style and structure of what you write. The rushing of rivers, the dazzle of flowers, the roots of trees, the buzzing of insects can all work to mold your mind. This act of attentive crafting might be the beginning of a nature rhetoric.

ঽ

Answer with one leaf a whole book of insults.
—modified from Lope de Vega,
sixteenth-century
Spanish poet

Practice photosynthesis by word.

ঽ

TERMES OF THE JAY

thou janglest as a jay
—Chaucer, *The Man
of Laws Tale*

AS DESCRIBED BY David Burnley in his book *A Guide to Chaucer's English,* one of Chaucer's great contributions to the English language was his recognition that this fledgling language had finally developed enough complexity by the late 1300s to allow for the partitioning of words into specialized vocabularies (i.e., sets of words and styles of expression that were unique to law, literature, love, etc.). Chaucer's brilliance as a poet lay in how he simultaneously played these vocabularies off each other, thus opening up the door for the development of refined literary modes such as allusion, allegory, and metaphor.

Central to this process was the ancient rhetorician's concept of *proprietas*—defined as 'appropriateness' or the way that special properties or characteristics properly fit a thing—in which *propria* are the elements peculiar to a group in which the members share certain traits. Medieval writers made the additional distinction that when these elements involved words or parts of speech, they would be called *verba propria* (what Chaucer instead called *termes*, in the sense of "technical terms").

Put more simply, *verba propria* refers to the fact that groups of people like lawyers, doctors, or scientists each have their own specialized ways of communicating within their own memberships. However, it also makes sense that these specialized vocabularies (consisting of "termes") exist outside of, and are separate from, the common words (the "common core") that make up the vocabulary of everyday conversation. It is the tension and interplay between technical "termes" and "common core" words that Chaucer fruitfully explored by structuring *The Canterbury Tales* around the interactions of pilgrims from different occupations. And, according to Burnley, it is the transfer of specialized terms into common usage that changes those words from *verba propria* into *verba translata* (akin to what we call "metaphor").

There is no reason why this conversion of technical terms into metaphors would not be as productive today as it was for Chaucer; consider the vast vocabularies of technical terms that are now available to metaphor-making artists. One possibility might be to play with and extend ("drawen on lengthe") the technical definitions of our relationships with nature. For example, the word *observe* could be lifted out of its narrow limitations as a strictly visual activity into an activity we do with other parts of our body. Or why not take scientific terms and extend them with new metaphoric possibilities; for instance, try using *hypothesize* as a verb for the behavior of an animal, or *photosynthesis* as an expression for the work you do when you read a book.

꙳

*Each of us has the potential to create small systems that lead
to ever-expanding fields of ideas contributed by other people.
For example, if you invented the concept of "1, 2, 3," it would
invite other people to continue adding "4, 5, 6, 7 . . . ."
Think about how a writer could do this with language.*

꙳

OVERSTEPPING BOUNDS

Word order is a "grammatical fiction."
—Northrup Frye

THE ROMAN RHETORICIAN Quintilian claimed that only
when we deviate from expected word orders does language
come alive with emotion and intensity, and many great writers have taken this advice to heart, with William Shakespeare
(*"Now will I to the chink"* etc.) being one prominent example.

The deliberate or dramatic departure from standard word
order, what classical rhetoricians called *hyperbaton* (literally 'to
overstep'), is a powerful tool because it helps highlight specific
words, ideas, disruptions, or turns in a sentence. In the hands
of a skilled writer, hyperbaton awakens language and fills it
with life. When Emily Dickinson writes "from cocoon forth a
butterfly," she throws *cocoon* into sharp relief, then releases our
minds on wings.

We have all been taught, and are constantly reminded, how
to craft grammatically correct sentences. And while such sen-

tences function in a strictly mechanical sense and are the ideal conduits of expression in an industrial society, we need to ask whether they are the right sentences for speaking of the power, subtlety, and rich beauty of the natural world. Inverted word orders take us outside—outside the boundaries of the expected—into a realm where forest black runs blue water and anything is possible.

&

a fragile—to the savage—he
entrusted—to the sea—a skiff

in the overwhelming—trembling—they
swam—in the water—deer
—Horace, first century BC poet

Toss aside all conventions for how sentences should look.

&

PLACE-NAME ELEMENTS

ONE OF THE MOST important functions of language is the naming of places. It is the primary way that communities and peoples know who they are in the world, and it is the first essential step in mapping out each person's personal, social, civic, moral, and religious universe. Yet in our modern age, where everything is mapped to microscopic detail and we are constantly surrounded by instant access to digitized maps, we have traded the creative act of naming places for the easy consumption of ready-made place-names.

Place-names may be labels as simple as *Fred's Favorite Tree* or *Abigail's Meadow*, but the true symbolic, creative, and ritual power of place-names is unleashed when place-names are made from new words or crafted in new ways. This is especially true when place-names are meant to carry symbolic or elevated meaning, as in the telling of mythic or moral tales. Yet ordinary English words have been normalized and commodified to the point where they no longer carry deeper meanings, so this work must be done with new words or new forms of old words.

J. R. R. Tolkien, who has been called the "godfather of modern language creation," was a renowned Anglo-Saxon scholar and philologist who turned his lifelong passion for language-making into one of the greatest epic stories of our time. Tolkien was a master at crafting unique place-names, and he populated his *Lord of the Rings* trilogy with an entirely invented and richly named world of fantasy. It is instructive and inspiring to examine how Tolkien created some of his place-names out of elements drawn from old languages and English dialects, as in the following examples:

Isengard a combination of an obscure English word for iron with the Germanic word *gard* 'enclosure.'

Middle-Earth an Old English compound, *middan-eard* 'middle dwelling, the abode of men'; appears in Middle English as *middel-ērd*.

Nobottle a combination of *new* and Old English *bold* 'building or dwelling.'

Oatbarton a combination of *oat* and Old English *beretūn* 'a courtyard or farm.'

Overbourn Marsh merges Old English *ōfer* 'edge, riverbank' with *burna* 'stream'; *bourn* is a common element in many English place-names.

Rushey a combination of the plant name *rush* with the Old Norse element *-ey* 'small island.'

Shire Old English *scīr* 'a district, province, or parish'; *shire* is also an English dialect word for 'a division of a county.'

Tolkien is here engaging in creative place-naming, and the same techniques are available to any of us. There are different ways to approach this process, but one model that I favor is using roots and stems as building blocks. To this end I have assembled lists of some word elements that might prove useful for naming places in the natural world.

These lists contain the core components of old Greek and Latin words that already form the basis of many Modern English words. For example, the first entry is the element *thym* (as found in the word *thyme*); this element is not a word by itself but is the core building block of a cluster of related Greek words including *thymelē, thymos, thymon,* and *thymus.*

These elements are offered as starting points or building blocks. And as building blocks they do not have standardized spellings and can be completed with different vowels or linking letters. For example, the element *cyan* has been variously written as *cyana, cyani,* and *cyano.* Likewise, the element *parv* has been used in words ranging from *parvus* to *parvitus,* and the element *xanth* has appeared in forms like *xanthella, xanthium, xantho,* and *xanthin.* (See the next section, British Place-Names, for more examples of how building blocks can be modified in the making of place-names.)

It should be clear from these examples (and encouraging to anyone thinking about creating place-names out of these elements) that there is no reason to worry about using these elements in a "wrong" way; even if you do create a word that is in some way deemed incorrect, then other users will correct your spelling in subsequent uses of the word.

In the following lists I have focused on elements that point to straightforward attributes, but you could also look through dictionaries (such as Jaeger's *Sourcebook of Biological Names and Terms*, or Borror's *Dictionary of Word Roots and Combining Forms*) and use roots and stems that suggest metaphorical meanings. For instance, the element *laena*, 'cloak,' could be used to name the way a forest cloaks the earth or the way darkness cloaks the innards of a cave.

Basic Features
    altar *thym*
    barrier *obic*
    border, boundary *fin*
    cave *gron, spel, speo*
    cleft, gap *hiat*
    column, pillar *styl*
    door, small opening *osti*
    dwelling place *hed*
    earth, ground *hum, tell, terr*
    entrance, passage *parod*
    field *arv, camp*
    fissure *chas, rim*
    forest *das, drym, sylv*
    foundation *fund, hed*
    gate-keeper *pyl*
    glen, wooded dell *nap*
    grove *als*
    heaven, sky, vaulted roof *aether, coel, uran*
    hill *bun, coll, deir, tumul*
    house *eco, oec, oic*
    island *insul*

lake *lac*

lookout, watcher *scop*

lurking place *phol*

meadow *limon, prat*

mountain *mons, mont, oro*

mud *lim*

path, track *hod, stib*

pedestal, step *bema*

place *loc*

ridge *ambon, carin, culmen, dirin, lir, ocr*

river *flum, fluv*

rock, stone *lapid, lith, petr*

rocky crag *rachi, scopel, scopul*

rocky hollow, bowl *catin*

roof *oroph, steg, tect, teg, tegul*

root *rhizo*

sand, sandy place *aren*

sea *hal*

seam, suture *raph*

seashore *act, littor*

slope *clin*

spring *pida*

standing *stat*

stream *nama, nasm, rheo, rhyac*

summit *acr, acron*

temple *nao*

thunder *bront*

tree *dry*

turning point *rhope*

valley *convall, vallis*

wall *pariet*

water *lymph*

wind *vent*

world *mund*

Color

black *mela, nigr*

blue *azur, cyan, lazul*

brown *brunne, fusc*

golden *chrys*

green *chlor, virid*

red *ruber, rubra, rubrum*

white *alb, canut, leuc*

yellow *flav, xanth*

Size

large *macr, meg, grand*

long *long, mec*

short *brachy, brev*

small *micr, parv, pumil*

tall *alt, procer*

Position

above, over *hyper, supra*

across *trans*

against *ant, anti, contra*

around *am, ambi, circum, peri*

at *ad*

behind *opisth, post*

below, under *hyp, infra*

between *inter, meta*

from *a, ab, e, ex*

near *anch, proxim*

within *end, intr*

Body Parts

anus *an, proct*

arm *brachi*

belly *ventr*

body *corp, som*

bone *oss, oste*

claw *chel*

eye *ocul, ops*

foot *ped, pod*

hand *chir, man*

knee *gen, gon*

mouth *ora, stom*

nose *nas*

throat *gul*

Modifiers

beautiful *asti, cal*

crooked *gaus*

elegant *facet*

erect *ith*

hard *dur*

hidden *celet, cryps*

marshy *elod*

pure *cathar*

rough *horren*

sad *lyper*

shady *ascio*

shining *argus, candid, clar*

smooth *aphel, calv, enod, glab, lubric*

soft *hapal*

solitary *erem*

spotted *bali, conspers, macul*

surface *chrom*

united *appos*

unsteady *astas*

To round out these lists we can add some of the suffixes used to show that something belongs to a place. Examples of suffixes used with common words include:

-*anus* as used in *American, fountain, human* (belonging to the earth), *pagan* (belonging to the countryside), *urban* (belonging to the city)

-*arium* as used in *aquarium, herbarium, terrarium*

-*ary* as used in *diary, estuary, library, sanctuary*

-*icus*, -*ticus* as used in *aquatic, domestic, public, rustic*

-*inus* as used in *alpine, divine, marine, peregrine* (moving between places)

-*orium* as used in *auditorium, equator, mirror, promontory, territory*

To this list can be added place-marking suffixes used in scientific terminology:

-a, -um, -us turn geographic names into adjectives

-acus turns nouns into adjectives meaning 'belonging to'

-alis, -atilis turn nouns into adjectives meaning 'found in a habitat'

-cola suffix that signifies an inhabitant of a place

-ense, -ensis turn place-names into adjectives meaning 'belonging to that place'

-enus turns nouns into adjectives meaning 'belonging to'

-estre, -estris used with nouns to mean 'dwells in a habitat'

-etus forms nouns signifying where a thing belongs

-oi case ending used to mark location in Greek

Place-Naming Practice

It is easy to become confused amid long lists of strange word elements like these, but the goal is simply to introduce word elements that already exist in English which could be used in the creation of symbolic or meaningful place-names. These elements could be assembled with different combining letters or punctuation marks.

For the sake of the larger culture it would be best to strive for clarity and harmonious sounds, but there are no rules in this exercise. By way of illustration, here are some playful variations on how place-names could be assembled from these elements. These contributions are not polished by use, and they stick out as oddballs because they do not fit into any known contexts or stories, but they provide a place to start.

chroma (surface)+*macul* (spotted)+*lith* (rock):
 chromaculith, ChroMacuLith, chrom'aculith

135

cyan (blue)+*nama* (stream)+*nao* (temple):
  Cyana-nama-nao, cyanama'nao, cyana·nama·naotura

rheo (stream)+*an* (anus)+*cyan* (blue):
  Rheanocyano, rheo:ano:cyano

mont (mountain)+*bront* (thunder)+*eco* (home):
  Mont-bront-eco

parv (small)+*celet* (hidden)+*catin* (rocky hollow):
  parvicelo-catino, Parva'celatina

cal (beautiful)+*hal* (sea)+*littor* (seashore):
  cal-hal-littor, calhallittal

erem (solitary)+*nas* (nose)+*stat* (standing):
  erem'nas'stat, Eremonasistat

vent (wind)+*vent* (wind)+*mont* (mountain)+*lyper* (sad):
  vent-vent-mont-lyper

lubric (smooth)+*stom* (mouth)+*asti* (beautiful)+*icus*:
  Lubric:stomastic

gon (knee)+*anti* (against)+*fin* (border)+*vallis* (valley):
  Gonanti'fin'vallis

I am treelocal
    roclocal
    stonelocal solid.

BRITISH PLACE-NAMES

AS MENTIONED in the previous section, the building blocks of place-names can be legitimately modified in all kinds of unexpected ways to create unique, local names. There may be no better example of this tendency than in British place-names, which are quirky and well documented, and have a rich history. Some of these old elements have been so thoroughly altered that they are now almost unrecognizable (the name *Eton*, for instance, is a combination of *ea* 'river' and *tun* 'town').

There is a significant body of literature on British place-names, not to mention an abundance of building blocks that can be used to describe nearly every nuance of a landscape. The two-volume dictionary *English Place-Name Elements* by A. H. Smith is probably the most comprehensive source, but it lists elements alphabetically, which makes it almost impossible to compare synonymous terms for slightly different aspects of a landscape. Margaret Gelling's book *Place-Names in the Landscape* is in some ways more useful because it groups place-name elements in thematic categories, allowing you to compare, for instance, terms for slightly different kinds of hills.

I encourage you to dive deep into this amazing vocabulary of place-name elements, but for the moment I want to focus on the surprisingly creative ways these basic elements have been modified in the formation of place-names. In the lists below I've selected a handful of Gelling's thematic categories, highlighted some representative elements within each category, and listed a few examples of the many ways these elements have been altered in the formation of place-names. These are real-world examples of places in Britain, so I hope they inspire you to be creative and playful in your own place-naming practice, no matter which elements you start with. Keeping these examples in mind, try referring back to the lists of elements in the previous section, and experiment with some new ways of modifying each element.

Rivers and Lakes

bece 'stream' Beckton, Colebatch, Cottesbach

broc 'brook' Brockton, Brotton, Broxfield, Fullbrook

burna 'stream' Auburn, Cranborne, Lambourn, Melbourne

mere 'lake' Delamere, Enmore, Fulmer, Mareham, Marland, Wetmoor

pol 'pool' Otterpool, Polstead, Poulton, Pulham

well 'spring, stream' Outwell, Walltown, Welham, Woolcombe

Valleys

cumb 'a short, wide valley' Compton, Horcum, Moulsecoomb, Ulcombe

dale 'valley' Crossdale, Dalby

denu 'long, narrow valley' Buckden, Croydon, Deanham

hop 'remote enclosed place' Cascob, Evenjobb, Harehope, Heyop, Hopwood

Hills and Ridges

beorg 'hill, mound' Barholm, Barrowden, Bearstead, Brackenborough, Broughton

camb 'comb, crest' Cam, Camshead, Combs

dun 'hill' Cowden, Downham, Dunwood, Haydon

hoh 'heel, sharply projecting piece of ground' Hoghton, Holland, Hoo, Houghton, Hoyland, Huthwaite, Sandhoe *hyll* 'craggy hill' Catte<u>hall</u>, <u>Hil</u>field, <u>Hul</u>ton, Wind<u>hill</u>

scelf 'shelf' <u>Shel</u>ton, <u>Shil</u>ton, <u>Skel</u>ton

Forests and Woods

bearu 'grove' <u>Bare</u>, <u>Bar</u>rasford, <u>Barrow</u>, <u>Beer</u>, Lark<u>beare</u>

fyrhth 'overgrown land' <u>Fir</u>bank, <u>Frith</u>, <u>Thrift</u>

graf 'grove' <u>Graf</u>ton, Hal<u>grave</u>, Rams<u>greave</u>, Short<u>grove</u>

leah 'forest' Ash<u>ley</u>, Oak<u>le</u>, Oak<u>leigh</u>

treow 'tree' Coven<u>try</u>, <u>Tre</u>borough, <u>Tree</u>ton, <u>Trey</u>ford, <u>Trow</u>bridge

wald 'forest' Cots<u>wolds</u>, Ring<u>would</u>, <u>Wauld</u>by, <u>Weald</u>

❧

this is where the earth is torn-aul-apart

❧

TEXTURE

ALONG WITH COLOR and form, texture is one of three important qualities that can be used to describe the surface features of physical objects. Our world is full of an astonishing variety of tantalizing textures that offer fertile ground for innovation and invention.

Consider the possibilities and limitations of Latin-based texture words such as *alveolate, lanate, fimbriate, strigose, papillate, puberulent,* and long lists of other words you will find in scientific glossaries. On one hand, these words open up some playful possibilities, but on the other hand these complex, multisyllabic words are limiting because they convey little to the imagination.

While *color* means 'that which covers' and *form* speaks of outward shape or appearance, *texture* alone connotes something that is fabricated or created. Think of how the Indo-European root *teks-* is used in words like *text* ('something woven from words') or *textile* ('something woven from fibers'), and be fearless in weaving your own words to describe texture.

Examples of Texture Words

In addition to conventional texture words such as *smooth, rough, warty,* and *silky*, there is an astounding body of highly specialized texture terminology in the scientific literature. As mentioned above, these scientific terms are beautifully wrought and worth looking at more closely, but few of them are likely to be useful for writers. Try playing with this terminology and see if anything might be modified or repurposed for your own writing.

Here are some sample texture words used by botanists (out of several hundred listed in J. G. and M. W. Harris, *Plant Identification Terminology,* and W. T. Stern, *Botanical Latin*):

aculeate covered with prickles

alveolate honeycombed

arachnoid with long, cobwebby hairs

asperous rough

bullate covered with rounded blisters

ciliate having a marginal fringe of hairs

crinite having tufts of long, soft hairs

favulariate finely ribbed in a zigzag pattern

glebulate covered in clumps of granules

hispidulous with tiny stiff hairs

laevigate shining or polished

muricate roughened with short, sharp projections

papyraceous with a paper-like feel

roridus bearing transparent dew-like bumps

scabrid roughened

sulcate bearing lengthwise furrows

tartareous with a rough, crumbling surface

verrucate warty with irregular projections

And here are a few of the many texture terms used in geology:

aphanitic very finely grained

botryoidal grape-like

brecciated broken fragments in a fine-grained matrix

euhedral crystalline structures with clear, sharp facets

graphic covered with lines or shapes that resemble writing

hyaline glass-like

mylonitic fine grained and compact

ooidose with tiny egg-like projections

schistose thinly flaking

specular producing a mirror-like reflection

vuggy marked with cavities

Heading in a New Direction

Rather than limiting ourselves to standard, worn-out texture words like *rough*, or struggling to find literary uses for sophisticated scientific terms like *asperous*, let us take advantage of a fantastic opportunity to create our own texture words.

To start with, there are hundreds of roots that could be the building blocks of new texture words (try digging through Jaeger's *Sourcebook of Biological Names and Terms* or Borror's *Dictionary of Word Roots and Combining Forms*). Here are a few useful roots:

acan(th) spiny

achn chaff, froth

aci pointed

aleur flour-like

alut leathery

amath sandy

aphel smooth

asper rough

aula(c) furrowed

azale dry

blenn slimy

bol(ax) lumpy

bom(us) a raised place

byss(us) finely threaded

carchar jagged

cer(ast) horned

chalar/chalast slack, relaxed

chaul(oid) with projecting teeth

chers dry

chori(um) skin, membrane

cladar brittle

cnest rasp, scraper

collod gluey

daul shaggy

drimy piercing, stinging

dros dewy

eri(o) woolly

farin coarse meal

fav honeycombed

fracid soft

glab smooth

glaphyr polished

glischr sticky

gyps chalky

hirsute/hirt rough, hairy

holc furrowed

hyph woven

idr sweaty, gummy, or resinous

ily muddy, slimy

lachn/lan woolly

lasi hairy, woolly

leur smooth, even

lim muddy, slimy

lip sleek, oily

lubric slippery, smooth

mal(ac) woolly, soft

moll soft

muricat pointed

muscid mossy

myx mucus, slime

notio moist

ogm furrow

onc a small bump or hook

oul/ul woolly

papul pimple

paspal millet, fine meal

pex woolly

phell stony ground

phol scaly

phorm woven, plaited

pil hairy, felted

pladar damp

plic braided, folded

po grassy

poc fleece

rastr with lengthwise scratches

rhyss wrinkled

scab(r) rough

scalen uneven, crooked

scobin rasp

scyt leather

seri silk

somph spongy

stict punctured

sulc furrow, groove

tener soft, tender

tere smooth

thraust brittle

toment densely haired

tort twisted

trich hairy

trychin ragged

undulat wavy

velutin velvety

viros muddy, slimy

xest polished

These roots may look foreign at first glance, but it is important to realize we already use many of them in words so familiar we hardly notice the roots anymore (e.g., *exasperate, rhinoceros, simplicity*). And once embedded in words, the roots may not even relate to texture anymore but instead convey a more figurative connotation stemming from the original sense of the root. For instance, *moll* ('soft') shows up in words like *mollify* ('to soothe') and *emollient* ('making less harsh'), while *azale* ('dry') shows up in the plant name *azalea* (on the mistaken idea that this plant grows in dry areas).

The creation of texture words from these roots usually entails adding a suffix to the end of the root (see below), but roots convey the same meanings whether they appear at the beginning, middle, or end of the words being created. Roots may also drop, change, or add letters in the course of being combined with other word elements (e.g., *pil* as used in *plush, collod* as used in *protocol, tort* as used in *tart* or *torment*).

The easiest way to create texture words is to convert roots or nouns into adjectives by adding modifying suffixes, creating a new word that says something has a texture suggested by the root or noun. For example, the root *sulc* becomes the texture word *sulcate* through the addition of the suffix -*ate*, while the noun *wave* becomes the texture word *wavy* through the addition of the suffix -*y*.

Here is a partial list of helpful suffixes:

-ac concerning

-acious tending to, abounding in

-al belonging to

-ant, -ent being

-ar like, of the nature of, belonging to

-ate, -atus provided with

-baere (Old English) productive of

-cund (Old English) of the nature of

-ed provided with, characterized by

-en made of

-escent beginning to assume the condition of

-ic of the nature of, pertaining to

-ig (Old English) see *-y*

-ine of or pertaining to

-isc (Old English) see *-ish*

-ish of the nature of

-lent full of, prone to

-oid having the form or likeness of

-ose full of, abounding in

-ous see *-ose*

-some (used to intensify the quality)

-sum (Old English) see *-some*

-y full of, having the quality of

The Art of Crafting Texture Words

Texture words are valuable but easily overlooked tools for describing the natural world. Many writers forget to *touch* the world because our culture prefers detached, mind-centered, visual information (e.g., color) and conceptual information (e.g., form). Perhaps for this reason, it is even a little difficult to precisely categorize texture, with many texture words blending into shape (*rounded*), appearance (*spotted*), or quality (*moist*). In fact, few words describe textures directly; instead, they use images of something else to create a sense of what textures might feel like, often by reference to familiar shapes or objects. This gives us words like *cottony* or *cloud-like*, even though such words simply say that a texture is "like cotton" or "like a cloud" rather than doing the creative work of naming the texture itself.

At this point, the writer could turn to relatively straightforward texture words, or else diverge into a highly creative realm of play. Common words range from standard choices like *rough* or *smooth* to descriptive choices like *cottony* or *warty*. Creative words, on the other hand, tap into the range of potential roots and suffixes to rename the world.

There are at least three ways to think about building texture words. They could be built around the modern names of physical objects; they could be built around older, root names of physical objects; or they could be built around descriptive roots. I invite you to think of other possibilities, but we will focus on these three options as a starting point.

For example, let us consider the toad, a familiar animal with dry warty skin, and see what it might look like to create words that describe the texture of this animal's skin. To start with, there are standard choices like *warty, rough*, and *dry* (or you could use standard scientific words like *verrucate*). These are all adequate choices, but you have already lost the battle if you stop here, so try naming the texture by referring to the object itself with words like *toad-like*. As mentioned above, words like *toad-like* are descriptive, but they do not awaken the imagination.

Things get a little more interesting if you take the object name and combine it with unexpected suffixes from the list above, thus coining new words such as *toadine, toadish*, or *toa-*

dacious. This might give you phrases like *toadine skin* (and since words frequently change over time by dropping letters, you could conceivably aim for phrases like *oadin skin* or *todin skin*).

Another option is to try adding suffixes to older words and roots. For instance, the Medieval Latin word for toad is the lovely sounding *batrax*, which lends itself to texture words like *batraxic* or *batraxish*, and the ancient Greek word is *phrynos*, which lends itself to texture words like *phrynic* or *phrynoid*. This might give you phrases such as *batraxic skin* or *phrynic skin*.

The third choice is to look away from the object and turn to a description of the texture itself. Following our toad example, we can pick a texture root from our list above and begin building around that root. For instance, we can take *scab* ('rough') as one of the roots that might describe the feel of a toad's skin. This opens up a highly productive field of creative options, including *scabeus, scabsum, scabisc,* or even *scaboad* (by combining *scab+toad*).

The point of this exercise is to demonstrate that in any given instance there are dozens of possible paths for describing the texture of a single object. Many of the combinations look foolish or are too cumbersome to be of much use, but the fact that you have so many interesting and unexpected choices is fantastic. Each of these new words could have a unique context where it completes a rhyme or a sequence of sounds in a carefully crafted sentence or verse. Each new word also has the potential to describe a unique texture: the wartiness of a toad versus the wartiness of a mushroom cap, or the feel of dry warty skin versus wet warty skin. All that matters is that any one of these new words, no matter how strange it looks at first, has the capacity to spring to life as soon as it is used in a memorable context—and this is the work of a writer.

How would the mountain be strong
if it could not endure the sun?

ROCK

ALL THE VARIOUS WORDS that have been used to point to rocks imply a kind of durability or hardness. This makes sense because rocks are the one object in nature least likely to change during your lifetime, so they serve as a foundation, a "rock of ages." In fact, in the ancient world, rocks and trees were the two objects that represented the highest principles of sacred truth (for instance, *tree* and *truth* derive from the same root).

lapis

> delapidated
> lapidary
> lapidify
> lapis lazuli

lithos

> batholith
> lithiasis
> lithograph
> lithosphere
> monolith

petra

> petrify

petroglyph
petroleum
petrolic

saxum

saxatile
saxeous
saxicolous
saxifrage

stān

stain
stand
stay
stein
stone

&

COPULA ABSENCE

ONE OF THE MOST abundant but overlooked elements of the English language is the little throwaway link we automatically insert between the subject of a sentence and the sentence's predicate expression. This link, called a *copula*, takes the form of a *to be* verb (including *am, are, is, was, were*), and it appears in the vast majority of all sentences. For example, in the sentence "The fish is in the water," *the fish* is the subject and *in the water* is a predicate expression that has been linked to the subject by the copula *is*.

But what is the copula's function? In his book *Becoming*

Animal, David Abram observes that *to be* is "a very active thing to be doing" and that our careless use of this powerful verb flattens the world, making objects passive and inert in our minds. When we become accustomed to seeing *beingness* as nothing more than a linking element in sentences, we stop investigating its qualities. We no longer ask whether the verb *to be,* as it appears in statements like "he *is* tall" or "the rocks *are* heavy," signals an active or a passive process.

Indeed, copulas have a limited range of functions: they can signal membership (as in "snakes *are* reptiles"), properties (as in "rocks *are* durable"), or identities (as in "that rock *is* a rock"). The verb *to be* may also be replaced by pseudocopulas such as *become, feel, get, look,* or *seem,* as when "I am sad" is restated "I get sad," "I become sad," or "I seem sad." But in every case it is worth asking to what extent copulas and pseudocopulas have been emptied of meaning and whether this creates an opportunity to think about language.

One path would be to follow Abram's lead and deeply investigate the qualities of beingness, to understand that the action of existing or being is "the moment of the world's unfolding," and that the verb *to be* is one of the most potent words in our language.

Another option is to try something that several of the world's languages do: take out the copula altogether (what linguists call *copula absence*). After all, the function of a copula is already implied by the relationship between a subject and its predicate, and even in the absence of a copula we intuitively assign the property of the predicate to the subject (in the statement "rock heavy" it is clear that we mean that the subject *rock* has the property *heavy* and we do not need to know that it "*is* heavy").

It is even possible that when we remove the distancing copula, the active quality of *beingness* might revert back into the subject. Thus, in our minds we would no longer visualize an inert rock, but a rock that has been linguistically activated by absorbing the missing copula. This new formulation "rock heavy"—with the copula absent but intuitively added by our imagination—might make the rock come alive again. The rock is now doing something—it is actively manifesting and expressing a quality—and this animating power of language is the greatest gift we can give the world.

༄

One problem is that our experience is mediated
by convention instead of "it could be."

༄

SEEING COLOR

COLOR (literally 'that which covers') drenches and paints every surface of every object around us, yet few people could list more than a few names for any one of the basic colors. There are, for example, dozens (perhaps even hundreds) of available names for the greens of our world. In his 1912 classic *Color Standards and Nomenclature*—the definitive handbook once used by museums to document the colors of museum specimens—Robert Ridgway presents page after page of green color swatches with lovely lilting names like *chromium, chrysolite, cress, deep sea-foam, deep turtle, jade, jasper, olivine, rainette, shamrock*, and *tight danube*.

Color names, whether they are technical or common names, can be playful and evocative as well as highly descriptive. H.

A. Dade's 1949 *Color Terminology in Biology* offers a bit of both: Latinate names like *bubalinus, fumosus, badius, electrinus, umbrinus, glauco-venetus, atrolividus,* and *lavendulus,* alongside popular names like *rose, peach, saffron, apricot, bay, hazel, fawn, pistachio, mouse grey, sky blue, lilac,* and *leek green.* Color names can be further classified with a host of modifiers such as *blackish, faint, bright, dark, unpolished, intense, glossy, dull, pure, pale, deep, dirty, tinged,* and many more. These begin to create an unlimited range of combinations to describe the nuances of countless colors.

With these options and opportunities in mind, try challenging yourself to utilize a greater variety of color words. For a start, consider several possibilities: we could draw from the wealth of available names, we could create new color names (especially from pieces of existing color terms), or we could think about color names in entirely new ways.

Into the Tapestry

As mentioned above, the spectrum of available color names is immense and largely untapped. For the scientific and naturalist communities there are standard references such as Ridgway and Dade, while specialized users such as artists, fashion designers, and industrial manufacturers each have their own color guides and dictionaries.

Consider, as one example, a sampling of the Latinate color names developed by G. W. Bischoff in 1830 and listed in William Stearn's book *Botanical Latin.* These terms are offered here as valid color names, as well as starting points for your own explorations with this colorful lexicon.

Colorless
hyalinus glassy
aqueus watery

crystallinus icy

diaphanus transparent

White

niveus snowy

candidus pure or shining white

eburneus ivory (white with hint of yellow)

argenteus silvery (white with hint of blue)

albus dull white

cretaceus chalky (dull white with hint of gray)

Gray

cinereus ash gray

schistaceus slate gray (gray with strong blue tone)

plumbeus lead gray (gray with metallic luster)

fumosus smoke gray (gray with hint of brown)

murinus mouse gray (gray with hint of red)

caesius gray with hint of pale blue

glaucous gray with hint of green

Black

ater pure black with no luster

coracinus black with luster

niger black with hint of gray

anthracinus black with hint of blue

piceus black with hint of brown

Brown

umbrinus pure deep brown

fuscus brown with hint of gray or black

badius chestnut (dull brown with hint of red)

ferrugineus rusty (light brown with hint of red)

cinnamomeus cinnamon (bright brown with hint of red and yellow)

rufus rufous (brown with strong red tone)

fuligineus sooty (dull brown with strong black tone)

hepaticus liver (dull brown with hint of yellow)

Yellow

citreus lemon (pure yellow)

auratus bright golden yellow

flavus pale yellow

luteus egg yolk (yellow with hint of orange)

ochraceus ochre (yellow with hint of brown)

fulvus tawny (dull yellow with hint of gray and brown)

lividus livid (yellow with strong tones of gray, brown, and blue)

ravus yellow with strong gray tone

Green

viridis pure green

thalassicus sea green (dull green with strong blue-gray tone)

atrovirens deep green with hint of black

flavovirens green with strong yellow tone

olivaceus olive (green with strong brown tone)

Blue

cyaneus pure blue

indigoticus indigo (deep blue)

azureus light or sky blue

caesius lavender (pale blue with hint of gray)

violaceus violet (blue with strong red tone)

lilacinus lilac (pale violet with hint of white)

Red

ruber pure red

roseus rosy (pale red)

purpureus purple (dull red with hint of blue)

sangineus sanguine (dull red with hint of dark brown)

coccineus scarlet (red with hint of yellow)

miniatus vermilion (red with strong yellow tone)

flammeus flame red (red with strong orange tone)

cinnabarinus cinnabar (red with hint of orange)

lateritius brick red (dull red with strong gray tone)

Out of the Tapestry

With the wealth of names already available there is probably little need to create new color names. It's true that colors could be named after local objects or features for the purpose of devising a unique local vernacular (in the model of *Sierra Nevada blue*), but otherwise the exercise of assembling names out of thin air feels somewhat random and runs the risk of stripping away the emotions that familiar colors evoke in readers.

One alternate strategy for creating new color names might be to start with bits and pieces of existing color terminology. For instance, the Latin elements *ex-* and *e-* refer to tingeing, so you could conceivably invent color names like *treexolive*, *grayexolive*, or *redexrose*.

This process could go in so many different directions that I won't focus on it except to offer a few other tantalizing examples such as *rub-apple-red* (from Latin *ruber*), *so-range of sunset and violet*, and *ulf gra* (the gray wolf of Eddic poetry). But examples in this vein verge into using color names in new ways, which is the focus of the passage below.

Retapestrating the World

Colors are such a vital part of our world that they continually invite us to weave them into our language. Yet the mere act of labeling a single object with a single color name feels incredibly limited. Is this the only endpoint that our language can achieve? Could color names conceivably work in other ways?

I was musing about color one day when I came up with an image of the sun in the sky as *disk in blue*. I tried running this together into *diskinblue* and saw the word *skin*, so I separated it to read *di-skin-blue*. But this made the word *skin* too strong and misleading, so I tweaked it again and ended up with the phrase "the color of *di-sk-in blue*." As a way of looking at colors in the world, *di-sk-in blue* is the kind of label that keeps tugging at my imagination with its eerie echoes of *dye, skin*, and *blue* bumping unexpectedly into each other.

This experience got me playing with color words in other ways. These experiments are not always successful, but they keep me thinking about color in the world, and that is a lot of fun. I have tried phrases like *died-in-blue, pushed from blue*, and *fores-blu-sky*. I have taken color phrases like *gray of sky* or *green of tree* and then pushed them to see if they could say something new with *gray-o-sky, graosky, grao-sky, green-o-tree, grenotree, greenotere*, and so on. I took the Latin word *comitia* ('an assembly or committee') and tried out *comitia of blue* for the sky and *comitia of green* for a meadow or forest. And I have wandered off into combinations like *redness-orange* or *the tawny side of yellow next to red* in search of other ways to put colors together.

A friend of the Roman poet Ovid once wrote in a poem that

a woman's arms were "whiter than purple snow." This image sounds odd at first, but it opens up another avenue for thinking about color because the purple of this poem was not a color but a Roman metaphor for the glowing vitality of youth. It is as if you wrote about the "gray arm of day," in which gray is not a color but a metaphor for the day reaching out to smother you.

Similarly, it is worth asking why we do not think of emotions in more colorful terms. We already associate colors with emotions in phrases like *I am yellow with jealousy*, *She is feeling blue*, or *He is seeing red*. But why stop at such simple phrases and associations? Why not push into new terrain like *yellous*, *poured-blue-anger*, *bluanger*, *bluad*, *violangerous rage*, or *sad-it-red*? Language-making processes open up countless avenues for describing color, and these are just a few suggestions. See if you can think of other ways to use color to paint your world with words.

"*I know new terms must be invented, since our tongue is poor, and this material is new.*"
—Lucretius, *De Rerum Naturae* (first century BC)

STATES OF MIND

IF YOU WERE ASKED to describe some psychological states of mind, you might come up with words like *sad, angry,* or *wistful.* But what does a word like *sad* mean? We can feel the emotion and we can visualize its effects on another person or on ourselves, but where is that state of mind out there in the world, and does this small word *sad* adequately represent the full range of sad-like emotions?

In fact it feels as if our vocabulary of psychology has veered toward such extreme simplicity that most of us could not list more than a few words to describe our emotions or states of mind. Undoubtedly things are easier this way, because with one word we can say "I love these socks," "I love this place," or "I will love my sweetheart forever and forever" without having to qualify the nuances of what we think we mean.

But the world is a far more interesting place than that, and everyone has access to these marvelous things called emotions. Therefore, we also have the power and capacity to explore and name these states of mind in any way we choose.

Consider how amazing it would be to develop a sophisticated vocabulary for psychological states of mind using natural images. Everywhere in nature there are moments ripe with potential for marking aspects of human experience that are far more subtle and complex than simple terms like *sad* or *angry.* For example, how about using the image of a seedling growing on the forest floor under the canopy of elder trees to signify a state of mind? Or the energy of wind rippling through tall grasses in a meadow? Or the sound of a single owl calling in the night?

This is not to say that poets and writers have not used nature images in these ways before, but it seems that these images are usually inserted into single poems or isolated in a narrative, rather than being used systematically and repeatedly as icons that grow with meaning over time. This is an important distinction because psychological states of mind are not something we invent to complement a particular rhyming scheme or to provide a convenient backdrop in a narrative thread. States of mind are vital aspects of what it means to be human, and these descriptive terms are meant to endure and be reflected upon by generations of thinkers.

So what about the words we use to describe our states of mind? The word *sad*, for instance, is an arbitrary word that signifies a powerful and universally felt emotion. It comes from an Old English word meaning 'sated, full,' which by some kind of metaphorical extension came to mean the emotion we associate with it now. But by the same token why couldn't another word, phrase, or image—even an image from the natural world—come to have the same meaning?

The use of natural images to signify states of mind opens up a wide range of new possibilities. For instance, "wind rippling over grass" does not have to signify anything other than 'wind rippling over grass'; it does not need to mean 'anger' or 'sadness' or anything else, it can just be its own unique and evocative state of mind. And why not have an emotion of "wind rippling over grass" or an emotion of "seedling under elder trees"?

And then, in the spirit of language-making, the real fun begins, because these phrases could evolve into their own new words. This might lead to expressions like *sedlin-under-elder* or *underelder*. Or *windingrass* or *ripplingrass* or *ripple-grass*. Imagine being able to say to your friends, "I'm ripplingrass today!"

The task as writer is to paint in words the feel of
a meaningful life well lived, to share the authenticity of
a well-worn haft in hand, the touch of something handmade,
the sounds of things that are real—words with real meanings,
songs of friends, the whisper of wind in a healthy forest.

WIND

IN HIS BOOK *Heaven's Breath*, Lyall Watson includes a glossary of nearly four hundred wind names from around the world—along with an enticing little note that English has "surprisingly few" labels for wind. We have technical terms like *gale* and some local names like *chinook*, but overall, as an almost daily fact of life, wind is largely overlooked in our language.

For anyone who thinks that a solution might be to toss in a few modifiers like "*strong* wind" or "*soft* breeze," it is instructive to consider the extensive naming schemes of the ancient world. We have scant knowledge of these traditions, but if the variety of names is any indication, then wind must have been an important and closely observed element in ancient Greek and Roman cultures. Named winds were identified with particular seasons and compass points, used to forecast expected weather conditions, and personified as deities or figures. Given that these were seafaring and agricultural civilizations, it makes sense that observing, understanding, and making offerings to the winds would have been a vital part of life.

Ancient peoples also noticed the obvious similarities between wind and the breath of living organisms. The Greek word *anemos* 'wind' later became the Latin word *anima*, which was applied to anything with a vapor, wind, or exhalation. It later came to mean 'life spirit' (that which "breathes life into" or "animates" a thing), while beings that possessed *anima* were called "animals."

The Greek relationship with wind was expressed in an astonishing variety of words that were used to describe many types of interactions with wind. A partial list of words derived from the root *anemo-* hints at a rich vocabulary that is absent in English. These Greek words are here translated as phrases because there are no equivalent words in English.

anemizomai driven with the wind

anemodartos stripped by the wind

anemodromos running with the wind

anemōkēs swift as the wind

anemōlia bazein speaking words of wind

anemoō exposed to the wind

anemosketēs sheltering from the wind

anemospharagos echoing to the wind

anemotrephēs fed by the wind

enchos anem reared by the wind

To these words can be added names for some of the characteristic winds that defined life in Greece. Many, but not all, named winds corresponded to points on the compass and were also personified. Other named winds include *Aeolus* 'ruler of wind' (derived from *aiolos* 'varying, unsteady'), *eos* 'the morning wind,' *etesian* 'annual winds,' and *zophos* 'the evening wind.' The following list is adapted from Watson.

Boreas the north wind, associated with cold rain and personified as an old man bearing a conch

Kaikias the northeast wind, associated with cold, wet weather and personified as an old man bearing a shield full of hailstones

Eurus the east wind, associated with hot, humid weather and personified as a well-dressed old man

Apeliotes the southeast wind, associated with gentle rain and personified as a young man bearing fruit

Notus the south wind, associated with hot, humid weather that brings rain and personified as a young man bearing a water jar

Lips the southwest wind, a strong wind personified as a young man holding the stern of a ship

Zephyrus the west wind, associated with mild, warm weather and personified as a young man bearing flowers

Skiron the northwest wind, a hot wind of summer personified as an old man bearing a pan of burning coals

The Romans had an equally elaborated system of naming winds for the points of a compass. Here is a brief list of basic names (also adapted from Watson), but keep in mind that additional words could be derived from each of these names, effectively creating an even richer vocabulary. For instance, *Auster* 'the south wind' formed other words like *austrifer* 'bringing the south wind' or *austrīnus* 'accompanied by the south wind.' In addition to these named winds are other categories like the *tempestates* 'the tempests,' powerful wind goddesses who had their own temples where sailors offered sacrifices before sailing.

Septentrio the north wind

Aquilo the northeast wind (also *Supernas* or *Gallicus*)

Carbas the east wind (also *Solanus*; or *Ornithias*, an east wind associated with the arrival of migrating birds)

Vulturnus the southeast wind (also *Subsolanus*)

Auster the south wind (also *Leuconotus*)

Libonotus the south-southwest wind (also *Altanus*)

Afer turbo the southwest wind (also *Africus ventus* or *Subvesperus*)

Favonius the west wind

Caurus the northwest wind (also *Circius*, *Argestes*, *Etesiae*, or *Thrascias*)

These lists are not necessarily definitive because both Greek and Roman authors seemed to delight in creating their own naming schemes. Instead, I offer these lists as suggestions for thinking about wind as a dynamic and varied presence in your own life. Each wind in the area where you live could be named according to its season, its associated weather, or its characteristic qualities. Does it arrive when you are planting the garden or when autumn leaves are falling? Is it a gentle wind tumbling loose papers down the sidewalk, or does it blast like a hot furnace? And consider your relationships with these winds. Do you lean into them and let them toss your hair about, or do you take shelter from them? Are there winds that *inspire* you or *animate* you?

§﹒

*A thing is lost when we can no longer find a way
to share our love for it with other people.*

§﹒

CLOUDS

CLOUDS ARE ONE OF the most consistently obvious natural features in the world, yet it is remarkable how few of us know or use the names of the ten basic cloud types. This is partly due to the arcane terminology favored by meteorologists since 1802, but spend some time with any field guide to clouds (*The Weather Identification Handbook* by Storm Dunlop is an excellent resource) and you might find yourself watching and reading the sky with a new sense of fascination.

Clouds are concentrations of water droplets or ice crystals that form whenever air cools enough to create condensation, either by coming in contact with cold ground or by rising into the colder upper atmosphere. Air rises in one of three ways: on thermals of hot air (convection), from being pushed up and over mountains, or by front lifting (when a mass of cold, dense air pushes under the leading edge of a lighter, warmer mass of air).

Most of us think of clouds as objects moving across the sky, but in fact the air that creates a cloud is constantly moving, and a "cloud" is simply an ephemeral phenomenon marking the points where air flows into or through colder pockets. Thus, a stationary cloud is like a grocery store checkout line: the phenomenon itself occurs in a single location, but the constituents creating it are constantly moving through.

Classifying clouds is a relatively logical process because they come in three distinct forms. *Cumulus* clouds are mostly rounded and broccoli-like on their upper surfaces, indicating atmospheric instability and active vertical uplift (convection). *Stratus* clouds consist of flat layers with smooth upper surfaces, indicating atmospheric stability. *Cirrus* clouds are curled and hair-like, formed by wispy trails of ice crystals being blown by strong winds in the upper atmosphere.

Within this classification there are ten genera (basic types) and twenty-six species of clouds, sorted by their height over the ground:

- HIGH CLOUDS have their bases more than 20,000 feet over the ground.

   Cirrus are fibrous wispy clouds, popularly called "mare's tails."
   Cirrostratus are featureless sheets of thin clouds.
   Cirrocumulus are tiny rounded clouds, uniformly white and showing no shading at all, with many clear gaps of blue sky.

- MEDIUM-LEVEL CLOUDS have their bases 6,500 to 20,000 feet high.

   Altocumulus are heaped and rounded clouds, with distinct gaps showing different shades of gray sky (but no dark gray).
   Altostratus are sheets of featureless gray to white clouds.
   Nimbostratus are broken dark gray clouds that often extend down to the ground to produce precipitation.

- LOW CLOUDS have bases that are less than 6,500 feet high.

   Cumulus are rounded heaps of clouds, often floating singly in a clear blue sky, and often marked by their flat bases.
   Stratus are featureless gray to blue-gray layers near or on the ground (fog), with soft formless bases and producing little or no precipitation.
   Stratocumulus are heaps and rolls of clouds with distinct gaps, showing sharply mixed grays including many dark gray clouds.

- TOWERING CLOUDS extend to many levels at once.

  Cumulonimbus are immense stacked clouds reaching to great heights with ragged bases, producing heavy precipitation.

Cloud Play

The desire to name clouds is readily found in our childlike wonder at spotting familiar objects and animals in the shapes of clouds. But despite the ubiquitous, overarching presence of clouds in our lives there are almost no synonyms and few etymological connotations associated with the word *cloud*. For example, *Roget's International Thesaurus* offers a pretty skimpy list of options—*woolpack, goat's-hair, messengers, scud, rack, mare's-tail, drisk, pea soup, haze*—few of which directly correspond with the generalized sense of "cloud."

Even the word *cloud* itself simply designates something that has mass, deriving from the old word *clud*—which could be used interchangeably to mean rock, hill, or cloud, and is akin to lumpish words like *clod* and *clot*. This term is so vague that it is as if our language has intentionally overlooked an object of tremendous variety and splendor. Wouldn't it be a lovely exercise to rethink these fluffy objects populating our heavens?

The formal scientific names for clouds offer some promising starting points. The language is beautiful (see above), but it is clear that few people have embraced terms like *altocumulus* and *cirrostratus*, so here is an opportunity to go back to the original roots or to wander the imagination in search of new images.

Cumulus, for instance, is related to the same root word as *cave* and *church*. And *stratus* has the sense of a paved road in the sky because it comes from the root *ster-* 'to spread,' as found in *street, strew*, and *stray*. Other charming linguistic links show up in the Old Irish word *strath* 'a wide river valley' or the Greek word *stroma* 'a mattress, bed.' Some of those billowing clouds sure look like *stroma* to me, and come to think of it, an awful lot of those clouds seem to be straying and strewn across the wide valley of the sky.

§॰

Language without honor is conceit.

§॰

SHALLOW NAME SONATINA

IN MANY WAYS, it is unfortunate that our paths into the natural world are mapped in the coded language of scientific nomenclature, and that we are asked to rely on a system of formal plant and animal names given to us and controlled by scientists. As described elsewhere, these "shallow names" should be thought of as placeholders in serious need of revision. Ideally, this would mean the radical re-creation of new names that arise from a deeper understanding of each plant or animal's life, or that arise from a richer cosmology of the natural world.

It is understandable, however, if a writer feels unable or unwilling to propose radical new names, so another solution might be to rename individual species through the less radical linguistic processes of clipping or blending. Thus, rather than entirely jettisoning common names like Brewer's Blackbird or Douglas-fir (both of which embody the old practice of naming species after prominent men), you might end up with "new" names such as *brewbird* or *dougfir*. In fact, a handful of abbreviated names like these are already used colloquially by field biologists, but I know of no examples that have become commonplace in written communication.

Clipping is a common word-forming process whereby parts of words come to stand for whole words or phrases. Clipped words may look strange when they first appear, but some become so familiar that users forget or no longer use the original words. Examples of clipped words would be *binocs* for binoculars, *dis* for disrespect, *flu* for influenza, *hyper* for hyperactive, *phone* for telephone, *radio* for radiotelegraphy. Clipping is not an exotic linguistic process; in fact it is a modern phenomenon that picked up steam in the twentieth century through the media of magazines and newspapers.

The most common strategy for clipping is to retain the first part of the original word, although clipped words can also be derived from the middle (e.g., *flu* from *influenza*) or from the end (e.g., *phone* from *telephone*) of their source words. Most clippings preserve one or two strong, meaningful syllables, but meaningless syllables may also be extracted and given meaning over time (e.g., *van* from *caravan*). Longer, more complex words can also be built from clipped words, giving us examples like *vanning* or *info-packet*.

Blending is a process of forming new words from the parts of two or more words. Common examples of blended words include *brunch* (breakfast+lunch), *motel* (motor+hotel), and *smog* (smoke+fog). This process seems to be particularly successful where components from the source words overlap in pronunciation or spelling (e.g., mo̲t̲or + ho̲t̲el). Blends are similar to and can include clipping to the extent that blends contain clipped words that have been joined to form new words. Another option is to blend the first letters of words to form acronyms, as in UNESCO, NATO, YMCA, UFO, or snafu (*situation normal all fouled up*).

Clipped and blended words typically arise in social situations where shared, long-term usage makes it possible to communicate clearly even when using parts of common words; this would make these words ideal within a community of people who share a passion for speaking of the natural world. Clipped or blended words are often faulted for having an air of frivolity, but they serve a vital social function by making communication within a group of people more succinct and efficient.

The processes of clipping or blending the common names of plants and animals opens up some intriguing ways to think about naming, though admittedly these processes may work well only for charismatic and widely referenced species. Examples already in common usage include colloquial names like *redtail* for Red-tailed Hawk, *coop* for Cooper's Hawk, *sharpie* for Sharp-shinned Hawk, and *coho* for Coho Salmon. Creating other new names will require a sense of playfulness, but examples of how these processes might work could include *sneg* or *snegret* for Snowy Egret, *cavi* or *cavire* for Cassin's Vireo, *weki* or *wekibird* for Western Kingbird, *gianquoia* for Giant Sequoia, *polepine* for Lodgepole Pine, and *osapine* or *pondo* for Ponderosa Pine.

It should be clear that clipping and blending are infinitely creative processes, so there is no reason to feel limited by these examples. Ultimately, these processes may or may not prove to be productive ways of responding to the issue of shallow names; they are simply one potential solution for taking ownership of the names you use.

&·

The triumph of science and logic is that they are one way to describe our world.

The failure of science and logic is that they strip out the magic and emotion that make life worth living.

&·

SPECIES AND IDEAS

WE THINK OF *species* as a term for classifying objects that exist in the physical world, but in fact this word comes from the same root word (*eidos*) and at one time meant pretty much the same thing as *ideas*, a term now reserved for immaterial objects that exist only in the mind (for a detailed exploration of this fascinating topic see *Dictionary of Untranslatables*, edited by Barbara Cassin).

The early Greek philosopher Plato first used the word *eidos* (meaning 'outward appearance or form') to describe the preexisting archetypal forms that he felt we perceived when we looked at any object. Thus, in looking at an oak tree we do not see an individual tree in the real world but an "ideal" oak tree that exists in our minds (of which the real tree is but an imperfect copy). Hence Plato's use of *eidos* transformed into what we call "ideas."

Aristotle, on the other hand, questioned the existence of free-floating, preexisting ideals and instead proposed that when we look at an oak tree we see the set of features which unites all oak trees. Hence Aristotle's use of *eidos* became what we call "species" (as in a group of individuals that share common traits).

Now completely separated in the way we use them, these terms actually have much in common and can profitably inform each other. What would it be like, for instance, to give internal "ideas" external "forms" in the natural world, and vice versa? Is the robust strength of an oak tree the outward expression of an idea in your mind, or can you turn this around and feel the oak tree within your ideas?

♠

*Our life on the trail, in the wild, is the fabric of what's
meaningful; it's the one story we can tell
where science leaves us empty.*

♠

BODY LANGUAGE

IT IS BREATHTAKING how often the ancient Greeks used
body images to describe the world around them, even as a
way of expressing otherwise unexplainable concepts such as
thought, consciousness, and *death* (many examples can be found
in R. B. Onians, *The Origins of European Thought*). The heroes
of Homeric epics, for instance, mirrored all aspects of their
life energy with their physical bodies, as when the heart of
Agamemnon is said to be filled to the brim with black anger in
Book 1 of *The Iliad*.

In modern times we have largely lost (or neglected) the
ability to view our bodies as active agents in the processes of
thinking, feeling, or expressing our sense of the world around
us; we have instead turned these processes into detached mental activities. Is it possible that creating new language could
help us reconnect our bodies to the natural world?

Try imagining some ways we could utilize our bodies as
tools for describing the world around us. What about using
body parts, either human or animal, as elements in compound
words? For example, we could add *hand-* to other words as an
element that suggests cupping, holding, or pointing: *we went
forth under a hand-cloud day.*

Or what about naming places after body parts? This could include direct naming such as Footshelter or Headspace, or using old words like Greek *pugme* 'the distance from elbow to knuckles' (origin of our word *pygmy*) as a source for new names.

Or how about extending the practice of finger rhymes and fingerplay already used by every culture in the world to teach infants? Finger rhymes could even be used as rhetorical structuring devices; for instance, you could develop a statement or description in five steps corresponding to the five fingers of one hand, elaborate or counterbalance the statement in five steps on the other hand's fingers, and then symbolically bring the two hands together for a conclusion.

Our bodies are our most basic instruments. They measure and reflect our world in the most vivid and dramatic ways possible, personifying and bringing life to an otherwise impersonal universe. We are *hu-man*, born of the earth, "earthlings"; let our language reflect this.

⁊

Sing the song of your heart laying itself upon the land.

⁊

PERSONAL PRONOUNS

PRONOUNS ARE SO ubiquitous in English that we scarcely pause to consider the ways they shape our perceptions and attitudes. In fact, pronouns are so widespread in the world's languages that they have been called one of "the most persistent elements in any language," and their use has been traced all the way back to the distant roots of English (see Mallory and Adams, *The Oxford Introduction to Proto-Indo-European and the Proto-Indo-European World*).

At the same time, each pronoun is a step away from its source; in other words, it is not the name of a person or thing but a more distant reference to that person or thing (as in "My friend Bob thinks *he* can climb that mountain."). This gap is particularly pronounced in the third-person pronouns—*he, she, it*—a fact noted by Émile Benveniste in his 1956 essay "The Nature of Pronouns," in which he states that only "the first and second person pronouns are 'real people'" and that "The third person [pronoun] is not a 'person': it is really the verbal form whose function is to represent the non-person."

In this context it is notable that third-person pronouns were absent in Proto-Indo-European, because this raises the question of whether we need third-person pronouns at all. What would it be like to use only first-person (*I, me, we, us*) and second-person (*you*) pronouns in your writing?

One reason for trying this out is to acknowledge that there are only two kinds of individuals in the world: *you* and *me*. Together *we* are the only people who can figure things out and build community. It's telling that in an exhaustive survey of Eurasiatic language families, the number one word with the most cognates was *you*, the number two word with the most cognates was *I*, and the number five word was *we*. If these linguistic clues suggest anything, it's that for thousands of years our ancestors recognized and honored the preeminent importance of first- and second-person pronouns while seeing no need for third-person pronouns.

So what happens if you shift your thinking and use only the personal pronouns *you* and *I*? Does your world feel any more personal and direct, or might problems be any easier to solve, if the only people in the world are you and me? What if we walk away from phrases like "He did that," "She did this," and "It is their fault"? What if we focus instead on phrases like "I feel this," "You can help me," and "Let us work together"?

I also like this shift to first- and second-person pronouns because it makes me think about playing with words in new ways. Take, for example, a simple Latin verb such as *venate* 'to hunt,' which might be used to form words like *ivenate* 'I hunt' or *uvenate* 'you hunt.' Or how about *ifeel* and *ufeel*, or *isee* and *usee*.

It's that simple: either I do an action or you do an action. We create this world together.

❧

*Awfishsensecyhawsnodingtoodoowid
(communication)
itsownleeawboutmahnee.*

*Are you speaking about the truth of something
in the world? (a constantive speech act)
Or saying something in order to change the world?
(a performative speech act)*

❧

CAPITAL PIRACY

ONE OF THE SHINING hallmarks of early Christianity was its remarkably elastic ability to co-opt and absorb the myths, images, and ceremonies of "pagan" cultures as a mechanism that rendered those cultures obsolete. The brilliant success of this strategy is one of the main reasons for the phenomenal rise of Christianity. With this example in mind, it might be time to turn this around and do the same thing to economic capitalism—to pirate and cannibalize the most revered icons and symbols of the corporate world in support of the natural world.

What would it look like, for instance, if we used words and images such as *stock portfolio, corporate executive,* and *mutual fund* to describe the ugliest and most pervasive "problems" in nature, everything from putrefaction and siblicide to toxic waste and deforestation? What if things that are horrifying, disgusting, and out of balance in nature were renamed as the icons glorified in the gilded suites of corporate headquarters? What if that swirling cesspool of industrial waste in the Pacific Ocean nicknamed the "Great Pacific Garbage Patch" was renamed the "Executive Boardroom"? What if dead animals along roads were called "stock options" or "layoffs"?

So what would be the point of this exercise? First of all, it would allow for some sly (yet serious) punning in the face of a monolithic monster. And it puts a real-world face on fancy terms designed to disguise what is nothing more than old-fashioned rape and pillage. "Stock options" and "mutual funds," after all, are merely corporate code words for the "conversion" (itself a code word to hide death and devastation) of earth resources and human lives into personal wealth.

We have to take responsibility for the words that are afoot in our culture. We cannot pretend that these words do not exist and simply wish they would go away; our best hope is to convert them into something else. What this something else looks like will be up to each writer, but it is clear that daily news cycles dominated by updates on financial markets and corporate deals will keep our culture captive until we find ways to alter the power and meaning held by each one of these words.

So have fun and see if you can match phrases from each column:

Cutting fins from live sharks	Profit statements
Pine beetle outbreaks	Bonuses
Fracking	Slush funds
Invasive species	Bailouts
Ivory poachers	Corporate retreats
Air pollution	Executive decisions
Strip mines	CEOs
Genetically modified crops	Board of directors
Oil spills	Boardrooms

The strong sometimes bloom larger than life in conceit.

fro olt ilt 'from all evil'
— *a fragment of the Lord's Prayer*
written in Norn (an ancient
Scandinavian language of
northern England)

GENDER OF ANIMACY

DUE TO THE CONSTRAINTS of our language, most English speakers recognize only two genders—*masculine* and *feminine*—though if pressed some people could name *neuter* as a third gender. However, in the world of languages this is an arbitrary simplification that profoundly limits our perception of gender.

As properly defined, gender is any type of category that helps speakers classify objects in their language. Gender categories can be based on almost anything—shapes, colors, ages, social functions, etc.—and while sexual identity is one potential type of gender, the word *gender* derives from the Latin *genus* 'a kind' (as in "a kind of") and has no sexual connotation at all.

Although there are many types, or potential types, of gender (i.e., categories), it is notable that the highly significant "gender of animacy" has been largely lost in English. Animacy is the category used in many of the world's languages to signal the degree to which an object is sentient or not. Even Indo-European, the ancestor of English, originally had separate genders for animate and inanimate objects, but later split the category of animate objects into masculine and feminine objects and increasingly restricted animacy to humans.

The streamlined gender system found in English may be elegant in its simplicity, but it leaves us few options for perceiving the life forces of different objects. We essentially have three choices in English: every object is either a masculine human (*he*), a feminine human (*she*), or a neutral thing (*it*).

Shadows of animacy persist in English, but not in any powerful way. We still distinguish between *who* when speaking of people ("Who is that?") and *what* when referring to inanimate or nonhuman objects ("What is that?"). We also distinguish between *who* ("This is the person who drank my milk") and *that/which* ("This is the animal that drank my milk").

But compare this to some of the more complex systems of animacy found in other languages. The Navajo language, for instance, does not simply recognize animate versus inanimate; it has a highly developed, eight-tiered hierarchy of animacy that ranks objects from most animate to least animate in an order like this: humans/lightning, infants/big animals, medium-sized animals, small animals, insects, natural forces, inanimate objects/plants, abstractions.

It's time to bring animacy back into our language for an important reason: it will be very difficult, if not impossible, to reanimate the natural world with a sense of spirit and sacredness if we are forced to use words already stripped of their capacity to signify animate life energy. A word like *rock* can never point to a sacred, meaningful, or life-filled object if the same word is used in sentences like "Let's crush up some rock to make this road." Reanimation requires new words, or new ways of signifying that familiar words now have new connotations.

Indo-European often had two different words for the same object based on whether the object was animate or inanimate. Many of these pairs have been lost or obscured by the great passage of time, but we can recognize one such pair in our words *ignite* (which developed out of the Indo-European word for any fire containing animate energy) and *fire* (which developed out of the Indo-European word for fire as an inanimate object). In this example, the old word for the animate object transformed into an active animating verb (*ignite*), while the word for the inanimate object became an all-purpose conventional noun (*fire*) with no linguistic features that convey deeper, spirit-based meaning.

It is important to note that animacy is not equal to personification (giving a thing personal or human qualities). In fact, it is telling that one definitive grammar book (*The New Fowler's Modern English Usage*) links the rise of personification to the demise of grammatical gender at the end of the Anglo-Saxon period. In other words, personification was invented out of necessity to fill the void after English lost its ability to speak coherently of animacy.

No matter what categories they signify, all gender systems become ambiguous and problematic when applied to the full range of objects in the real world. Consider how the masculine/feminine definite articles used in German, French, and Spanish (e.g., *el* and *la*) end up being arbitrarily applied to huge numbers of objects that have no inherent sexual characteristics. For example, "the sun" is masculine (*el sol*) in Spanish but feminine (*die Sonne*) in German, while "the moon" is feminine (*la luna*) in Spanish but masculine (*der Mond*) in German.

For this reason, it might not make sense to devise sweeping new grammatical rules for applying animacy to the English language. However, it does seem useful and important to begin designating animacy on a case-by-case basis when reinvestigating the life energy of formerly overlooked objects in the natural world. It makes sense, for instance, to start by naming special trees, rocks, mountains, valleys, or rivers as animate objects, and then over time begin marking animacy in words for other objects that speakers care about.

Many different processes have been used to mark gender (and animacy). Some languages use different words for different genders (e.g., *ignite* vs. *fire*). Some use pronouns (e.g., *he, she, it*). Some use unique prefixes or suffixes (e.g., *-ess* is a feminine marker in English, while *-or* is usually a masculine marker: *actress* vs. *actor*). And some languages simply change a few letters (e.g., *he* vs. *she*, or you could invent an example like *fire* vs. *fere*).

What's most important is that we experiment with ways to signal the vital animate energy that resides in objects now dismissed as "inanimate." The reason for doing this is to highlight objects and situations that can then be deepened with your awareness of their living energy or spirit. Only when you diverge from the rigidly bound, utilitarian gender imposed by conventional words can you begin to open up space for the world's magic.

If we bear dark brooding monsters we will live like storms.

TABOO NAMES

INDIGENOUS PEOPLES who live close to the land or rely on hunting for their livelihoods often have powerful taboos against speaking the names of animals or spiritually charged objects. These taboos are particularly relevant in hunting cultures where the uncertainty of finding food animals means that hunters have to avoid offending the spirits of those animals.

Instead of saying these names openly, it is often permissible to use replacement names that are not taboo. Shadows of these old traditions endure even in Modern English, though they are obscured by the long passage of time. A classic example is the animal name *bear*, which simply means 'the brown one.' Bear is a very old replacement (non-taboo) name for an animal of great significance to early European hunters, and some form of the word *bear* or other replacement names can be found in all Indo-European languages. Other examples of old replacement names include *lobo* (for the animal we now call "wolf"), *alopex* (for "fox"), and *ophidian* (for "snake").

Even when the potency of taboos is lost, an aversion to directly naming certain objects or topics still persists in all cultures, including modern societies. However, instead of deeply felt, powerful taboos, replacement names in modern society take the form of euphemisms, which are merely banal, secularized versions of taboos.

Euphemisms are innocuous words or phrases used to replace words that are considered offensive or harmful in some way. Unlike in traditional societies, where many important taboos are centered around food animals or highly charged places, perceived offenses in modern societies tend to be centered around sex, excretion, and religion. Therefore, we end up with euphemisms like "Jeez" or "Jiminy Cricket" for *Jesus*; as well as "SOB," the "F-word," and "frickin" for other words we try to avoid.

But no matter how you look at them, taboo replacement names and euphemisms will always be opportunities for language-making, because by "speaking around" or replacing objectionable words they lead to the creation of new words or new word meanings. Even if the replacement is little more than an acronym for the original word ("SOB") or is a deliberate mispronunciation ("frickin"), it still represents a productive, language-generating process.

Although modern societies favor secularized euphemisms, I find myself drawn to taboo replacement names because they are an aspect of peoples who actively practice deep reciprocal relationships with the sacredness of their world. It is hard, if not impossible, for a citizen of the modern world (detached from the never-ending quest to secure food in a wild environment) to truly understand just how vital these reciprocal relationships are for our survival, or how important it is to observe and honor these relationships.

As Richard Nelson writes in his astonishing book *Make Prayers to the Raven*, the Koyukon people of central Alaska emphasize that "The animal and its spirit are one in the same thing. When you name the animal you're also naming its spirit. That's why some animal names are [taboo] ... because calling the animal's name is like calling its spirit." As with other traditional peoples, the Koyukon claim that calling attention to an animal in an overt or disrespectful way can insult that animal's spirit—both as an individual animal and collectively as a species—and insulted animal spirits might exact vengeance or significantly alter a hunter's success.

This may sound hypothetical or arcane from the comfort of your living room, but it would feel a lot more urgent if you were hunting by yourself, deep in the vast wilderness of Alaska at forty degrees below zero, with your family starving at home. All of a sudden, that moment when you pointed your finger at a caribou or boastfully spoke its name might come back to haunt you. As Nelson quotes one Koyukon hunter, "The country knows. If you do wrong things to it, the whole country knows. It feels what's happening to it."

That is why it is important to speak carefully when using animal names—to say "the brown one" when telling a story. The Koyukon also do not name a bear directly; they have a replacement name that means "the black place," which we could render as *nigriloc* in the roots and stems of English.

Because there are very few, if any, taboo or replacement names related to nature that still carry power in English, this opens up an opportunity to start thinking about new names. Even if these names already existed they would still be open to change because it is the nature of these names that they lose their euphemistic value over time and need to be replaced (for example, the euphemism *privy* changed to *toilet* then to *water closet* and recently to *bathroom* and *restroom* as each previous term lost its value). The entire field of taboo names and replacement names in nature has been overlooked in modern times. Let us honor once again this tremendous language-generating potential.

If one goal of language is to elevate ideas, to lend them depth and texture, then it will always be a meaningful exercise to give words multiple meanings.

"*There are traces of meanings not wholly invented by us.*"
—Robert Bringhurst, *The Tree of Meaning*

THE MANY FACES OF SYNONYMS

LINGUISTS GENERALLY agree that no two words are exact synonyms, though some words come pretty darn close by replacing each other in many but not all sentences. However, it is one thing for two or more words to describe the same object or quality (to have the same denotation), while it is much more difficult for them to have the same expressive or social meaning (connotation). It is these slight differences between synonymous words that are gold for poets and writers, because these differences allow for stylistic variation. In other words, divergent or slightly divergent meanings in synonyms allow for precise and very subtle forms of expression.

Synonyms are easily overlooked, but they are a surprisingly dynamic aspect of language because the presence of a word will often actively block or restrict the creation and use of other words that have overlapping meanings. After all, why does a language need multiple words to signify the same thing?

Furthermore, this tension makes the relationships between synonyms inherently unstable because words with overlapping meanings will maneuver for supremacy over each other or challenge each other to assume new meanings.

But if synonyms seem unnecessary, they are still very common. For instance, Old English is notable for having many interchangeable synonyms—the epic poem *Beowulf* alone has twenty synonyms for the word *man*, and there are no clear reasons why one synonym was preferred over another in any given context (as a whole there are around thirty synonyms for "man" in Old English).

So why don't we include synonym-formation as part of our language-making toolkit? What happens if we create ten to twenty interchangeable words for things like trees, mountains, and birds?

A language typically responds to synonyms in one of three ways that help keep the language supple, flexible, and agile. It might test the synonyms over time and pick the word (or words) that work best for the language community. It might differentiate synonyms by using them to define increasingly subtle aspects of the same general meaning. Or it might split off synonyms and assign them new meanings altogether.

In all cases, a surplus of synonyms is the first essential condition because redundant linguistic material must be dealt with in some way. The task of a writer is to generate this abundance so that your language has some juicy material to work with.

Forms remain constant while meaning pours into them and keeps on flowing.

FORM

WHEN WE USE language to describe the world around us much of our effort goes into pointing to the physical objects we perceive with our senses, and it makes sense that we describe these objects according to their most obvious external features: texture, color, and form.

In his monumental, multivolume work *A History of Greek Philosophy*, W. K. C. Guthrie observes that the discovery of "form" may be the ancient Greeks' most singular contribution. Prior to this discovery every object was viewed as an individual entity; therefore, every single pencil would have been a separate, unique pencil and there would have been no broad category called "pencils" or "pencil-like" objects. The Greeks eventually realized that objects could be grouped by their shapes or other qualities and then named according to their *eidos*; in other words, an abstract "pencil" could now stand for all pencils.

In the works of Homer this Greek word *eidos* simply meant 'what one sees, shape,' and it referred to the basic physical properties of a person or object. But then philosophers got involved and things became really complicated, with Plato proposing that *eidos* referred to abstract ideal forms (what we now call "ideas") and Aristotle proposing that *eidos* referred to actual things that could be perceived and measured in the real world (what we now call "species"). The ensuing debate about the materiality or immateriality of "form," along with the corresponding Christian debate about existence versus essence, occupied the attention of nearly every great thinker from the time of ancient Greece through the Middle Ages.

It is not necessary to trace the nuances of this contentious history because we are focusing, at least as a first step, on the simple act of creating words for basic forms. It is these words, along with words for textures and colors, which will help us describe the physical world of nature in new ways.

Here then is a list of a few Greek and Latin roots that can be used to describe forms. There are root words for practically every object in the world, but I have tried to pick roots for generalized shapes like "round" (*gyr*) or "circle" (*circ*). These roots can be applied to almost any type of object and should be more productive than roots that only point to specific objects such as "hawk" (*aesal*) or "mushroom" (*agaric*). Some objects are so archetypal that they seem like universal forms ("tree" comes to mind), so there is plenty of gray area between forms and objects, but rather than worrying about this distinction I will just offer some roots and get the ball rolling.

The roots listed here are adapted from Jaeger's *Sourcebook of Biological Names and Terms*, and many of them look pretty strange at first glance. This is partly because Jaeger collected roots used in technical terms that are unfamiliar to most people, but it is also because we seldom recognize roots even when they form the core of common words. Consider for example the roots I've listed for "circle," including *circ, cycl, orb*, and *rot*, which are at work in words like *circular, cycle, orbit*, and *rotund*. A more subtle example might be *ocr*, one of the roots for "summit," which shows up in the word *mediocre* ('between summits' or 'medium-sized summit'). The latter example also shows how roots related to forms or objects can be used metaphorically, which greatly expands the expressive power of these roots.

But again, the roots listed here are merely starting points, and if you find them too technical or too obscure then do some research and find roots that work for you. For example, Donald Borror in his *Dictionary of Word Roots and Combining Forms*, John Kennedy in his *Stem Dictionary of the English Language*, and Eric Partridge in the appendix to his *Origins: A Short Etymological Dictionary of Modern English* each interpret and present roots in different ways.

Keep in mind that no matter how strange a root looks, it is a root exactly because it can be (and has already been) used to form words. Consider, for example, the root *cycl*. If you had never seen this root before, it would be hard to imagine that it could be used in a word, yet we use it in familiar words like *bicycle*, *cyclic*, and *cyclone* without giving it a second thought. Similarly, it is hard to imagine how to use an unfamiliar root like *orygm*, but the magic comes from finding ways to give this root new life in new words. Your task is to create words that everyone starts using, whether the roots look strange or not.

angle *agost, anc, angul, gon*   (<u>anc</u>hor, <u>angul</u>ar, poly<u>gon</u>)

arrow *sagitt, toxeum*   (<u>sagitt</u>arius)

ball *glob, pil*   (<u>glob</u>e, <u>pil</u>e)

bent or curved *ancyl, camp, cyph, flex, gamps, gaus, pand, scamb, scoli, strept*   (<u>flex</u>ible, <u>scoli</u>osis)

berry *bacc, cocc*   (<u>bacc</u>helor 'laurel berry')

bow *arc*   (<u>arc</u>her)

box *caps, cist, scrin, thec*   (<u>caps</u>ule, <u>cist</u>ern, <u>thec</u>a)

branch or shoot *blast, clad, clon, ram, thall*   (<u>clad</u>istics, <u>thall</u>us)

chain *caten, halys, orm, seir*   (<u>caten</u>ation, <u>horm</u>ogonium)

circle or ring *annul, circ, cycl, orb, rot*   (<u>circ</u>ular, <u>orb</u>ital)

club *clav, coryn*   (<u>clav</u>ate)

collar *cingul*   (<u>cingul</u>um)

cup *amby, calic, cyath, cylic, cymb, depas, manes, poteri, scyph*   (<u>cymb</u>al, <u>scyph</u>ozoan)

egg or oval *o, oo, ov*   (<u>oo</u>cyte, <u>ov</u>ate)

flattened *petal, plan, plat*   (explanation, plateau)

forked *dicr, furc*   (dicrotic, bifurcate)

formless *amorph, asem*   (amorphous)

fringe *fimbr, lom*   (fimbriated)

hair *crin, pil*   (crinoline, pilose)

heap or mound *agger, bun, sor*   (exaggerate, bunch, sorus)

hook or hooked *ham, harp, rhamph, unci*   (hamate, harpoon)

keel *carin*   (carina)

lentil-shaped *phac*   (phacofragmentation, phacoid)

lip *lab*   (labial)

net *arcy, dicty, ret*   (reticulate)

nipple or pimple *papill, papul, thel*   (papilla)

oblong *paramec, scut*   (paramecium)

pedestal *basid, scap*   (scape)

pipe or tube *aulon, cann, fistul, ochet, syring*   (cannon, fistula)

pit or hollow *alveol, areol, cav, cotyl, lacun, phreat*   (cavity, cotyledon, lacuna)

point or pointed *aci, cusp, epacr, mucro, spic, stigm*   (acid, mucronate, spicule, stigma)

round or rounded *gyr*   (gyroscope)

saw-edged *serr*   (serrate)

sickle *falc, zancl*   (falcon)

spoon *spath*   (spatula)

squared *quadrat*   (quadrangle)

star *aster*   (asterisk)

strap *chalin, haben, himant, lor*   (lore, the space between a bird's eye and beak) summit *acr, apic, culmin, ocr*   (<u>acr</u>obat, medi<u>ocr</u>e)

sword-like *acinac, glad, sagar, xiph*   (<u>gl</u>adiator, <u>gl</u>adiola, <u>xiph</u>oid)

thorn *acan, scol, sent*   (<u>acan</u>thus)

thread *fil, stamin*   (<u>fil</u>ament)

tree *arbor, dendr*   (<u>arbor</u>eal)

triangular *trigon*   (<u>trigon</u>ometry)

wing *ali, pter, ptil*   (<u>ai</u>sle, <u>pter</u>odactyl)

both rein and call shall be of value

FORMULAS

FORMULAS ARE STOCK phrases used repeatedly over time, with little or no variation, which work to carry the themes that matter to a culture (e.g., "In God We Trust"). In modern times such phrases might be called clichés, with the implication that repetition is somehow trite or shows a lack of originality. But in older cultures these oft-repeated phrases served as powerful poetic tools that delighted the ears of listeners and signaled the presence of key symbolic or transformative moments. As such, these "trite repetitions" can be the key foundation points from which thoughts arise rather than mere parking places where the mind pauses briefly during a longer narrative.

Formulas may occur in every type of text from simple chants to major mythic tales. An example of a common ancient

Indo-European formula is the phrase "may the land grow and prosper," and there are hundreds of other examples that can be classified according to categories detailed by Calvert Watkins in his book *How to Kill a Dragon*. These categories are useful because they suggest a framework for the creation of new formulas.

The simplest category includes formulas that spell out an *argument plus its negated argument* (for example, "sky that is blue and not blue," "land plowed and unplowed") or an *argument plus its counterargument* ("rivers fast and slow," "beasts hungry and full"). These "quantifying" formulas are used to signify the totality of an idea; i.e., all beasts, all rivers, all lands.

Formulas that consist of an *argument plus its negated counterargument* ("rivers fast and not slow," "beasts hungry and not yet full") or an *argument and a synonymous argument* ("rituals and chants," "stars and heavens") are called "qualifying" formulas because they intensify an idea.

More complex formulas include *kennings*, in which two nouns with no surface connection are taken together to signify a third notion or metaphor. Kennings were used prolifically in ancient literature, especially in Nordic literature, and included phrases such as "horses of the sea" (ships), "milk of grain" (ale), and "shepherd of the people" (king).

Merisms are similar to kennings except that the two nouns are more closely linked and when taken together signify the global group to which they belong. Thus "trees and flowers" could stand for all plants, and "beasts and birds" could signify all animals.

Categories aside, it is important to remember that formulas contain a lot of power, especially when used to convey deeper ritual or symbolic notions. Used singly or in a scattershot fashion they lose much of their meaning, but when formulas are skillfully repeated or arranged as signposts they may serve as potent narrative markers.

INVOKE, EXTEND, and AMPLIFY the motifs of folklore and myth but give them new forms and characters.

PARALLELS AND ECHOES

WHENEVER LETTERS, sounds, words, phrases, or verses are repeated in a poem, song, or text they inevitably create parallels and echoes. These parallels and echoes have what is called an "indexical function"; they first call attention to themselves and then point to a key poetic message (as if pointing with an index finger). And because repetition may strike a musical rather than logical note, it can lift language out of the realm of the ordinary and unmoor words from their safe harbor in the rational mind.

Repetition may be playful, as in a children's rhyme, but it is much more than wordplay. It is a powerful narrative tool that can be used to construct coherence and unity while at the same time exposing contrasts and disruptions in ideas or emotions. Repetition can be used to bring together elements that seem unrelated on the surface but inform each other at deeper levels, and one of the most significant roles of repetition is to mark text that requires and rewards increased attention so that these deeper levels can be revealed.

Repetition can occur at any level of language: it may involve individual letters or sounds; it may play out through words, clauses, sentences, or lines; or it may form textual structures and patterns that weave throughout a long narrative or poem.

And although we notice and focus on the units that are repeated, it is the distance and timing between repeated units that creates emotional power. These spaces build tension, flow, expectation, and disappointment—the rhythmic heartbeat of a text. When we scan a line of fence posts we tend to focus on the posts even though the intervals between the posts are just as important. If the pattern of spaces suddenly changed, we would immediately notice the change even if we only think of it in terms of the posts.

Repetition opens up space in another way too. As soon as our minds become accustomed to an expected pattern, we anticipate and automatically fill in the repeated units even before we encounter them, which means that a writer can use those spaces to further develop or elaborate a theme or idea. An example would be the traditional Christmas carol "The Twelve Days of Christmas," where the repeated pattern creates space for the singer's "true love" to offer a new present each day; another example might be the highly repetitive song "Ninety-Nine Bottles of Beer (on the Wall)," where the space is filled by a countdown of beer bottles.

One similar, and very ancient, strategy is referred to as "Behaghel's law of increasing terms." This refers to the addition of an epithet, or extra information, to the last member of a parallel pattern: *A+B+epithet C*. This looks like "mommy, daddy, and their little baby" but played out in sacred hymns, ritual chants, and poetic formulas (as in the confessional prayer *mea culpa, mea culpa, mea maxima culpa* or the Christian Trinity *Father, Son, and the Holy Ghost*). The injection of extra detail is even more compelling if placed next to a textual boundary (the end of a verse, phrase, sentence, or metrical unit); this privileged position further highlights the pattern.

Making an Echo

Parallels and echoes are a universal feature of highly crafted poetic language, so it makes sense that there is an extensive vocabulary for identifying and naming the many complex levels at which echoes operate. I can focus on only a few categories here, but I hope this will be enough to illustrate some of the diverse ways that repetition has been used.

Doubling is one of the simplest forms of repetition. Ancient Greek writers, for example, would often alter words by artificially doubling consonants, thus lengthening the sound of those consonants in order to make a word's meaning more pronounced. In the English tradition, Chaucer did this with emphatic and expressive words like *refressh* ('to refresh') or *ravisshe* ('to ravish'), and we could do something similar by adding an extra *n* to *sinnging* or an extra *g* to *angguish*. There are many ways that words for the natural world could be doubled like this too: how about using the expected word *run* for the running of two-legged animals, but substituting *runne* for the running of four-legged animals?

Letters can also be repeated across adjacent or sequential words. For example, the technique called *alliteration* was used extensively in Old English poetry. This repeating of initial letters (or sounds) helps stitch lines together in the same way that many Modern English poems are stitched together with rhymed words at the ends of verses. One analysis found that alliteration has been a far more popular and persistent poetic technique than word rhymes in the world's poetic traditions, and the enduring strength of alliterations can be observed in the long-term persistence of English phrases like *topsy-turvy*, *fit as a fiddle*, or *down in the dumps*.

Not only letters and sounds can be repeated, but words as well. The repetition of the same words or phrases at the beginning of successive units is called *anaphora*, and this technique figures prominently in the Bible, the *Epic of Gilgamesh*, and many other great works. Anaphora works by tying sections of a narrative or poem together, while at the same time asking the reader to carefully reevaluate the repeating pattern from different points of view. This can either build a drumbeat of momentum or slow things down by circling the narrative back to the same point over and over again. At an extreme, an overwrought anaphora leads to the loss of meaning as a word or phrase is used so many times that it starts to call attention to its own artificiality. This can be a serious drawback, or it can add more layers of meaning to a text.

Another technique used in ancient ritual literature was repeating a verb in subsequent verb phrases. In *How to Kill a Dragon*, Calvert Watkins cites examples from ancient Greek, "when a lion overpowers [a boar] the lion overcomes him by his power" and "heaven yearns to wound the earth and yearning seizes earth," and from Latin, "to purify and perform the purification."

The patterning of words in repeated structures was further developed as the highly influential technique of dividing choral lyrics and poems into *strophes, antistrophes,* and *epodes*. These predictable, three-tiered patterns initially served as memory aids for the oral performance of long narratives, but they also helped audiences interpret and respond to the performance. These patterns were so successful that divisions into strophe, antistrophe, and epode have been used as a traditional technique for over two thousand years.

A more expansive form of repetition is the special technique called *ring composition*, in which the beginning and ending points of a statement, discourse, or narrative mirror each other by repeating the same (or equivalent) words, phrases, or sounds. The basic strategy of a ring is to enclose and highlight "a narrative within the narrative." This extremely important technique is covered in greater detail elsewhere in this book.

Finally, repetition can take on far more subtle forms if the parallels and echoes are expressed through nonrepeating (different) elements. Dyads, for example, are pairs of words that parallel each other but are not equivalent and may or may not be opposites. The elements of dyads such as *night and day, green and brown, thunder and lightning, father and mother, silver and gold, heaven and earth,* and *land and sea* echo each other while helping tie larger ideas together. If dyads develop into traditional devices, as they often did, they can evolve into formulas and take on added layers of poetic or ritual meaning.

Watkins points to instances where the relationships between the elements of a dyad are further elaborated by sounds within the words. Examples include an Old Irish dyad that combines *dúan* 'poem' with *dúas* 'payment for a poem'; an Irish dyad with *clú* 'fame' and *cnú* 'nut, jewel' (as a metaphor for a reward); and an ancient Greek dyad with *nīkā* 'victory' and *tīmā* 'honor.' The last example is especially sophisticated because the vowels of this dyad mirror each other exactly while the properties of the consonants are reversed (the sequence *n-k* in *nīkā* is nasal sonorant-voiceless oral stop, while the *t-m* in *tīmā* is voiceless oral stop-nasal sonorant).

A lovely example for closing up this section on parallels and echoes is the technical name for ring composition in Irish. The term *dúnad* derives from *dún* (a circular stone structure in ancient Ireland), and this elegant little word repeats in its form what it signifies—a circle of letters (*d→d*) that closes back into itself, a tiny narrative within a larger narrative. In this one word we can see how parallels, echoes, and repetitions call up the past, mirror the present, and suggest the future while adding emotional power and great beauty to language. These are tools that could be used in everything you write; these are tools that could take a lifetime to master.

⟨❧⟩

Samsara
praise over praise over praise

⟨❧⟩

CATALOGS

IN EPIC LITERATURE a catalog is an encyclopedic list of items inserted into the midst of a larger narrative. Even a simple list of names can be a surprisingly powerful narrative tool, and many kinds of lists appear in ancient stories, including in both of Homer's epic tales *The Iliad* and *The Odyssey*. A list might be sparsely constructed with items only loosely related, offering little more than a "relationship of accumulation," or a list might be complexly elaborated and linked together with details and small vignettes (for a variety of examples see Benjamin Sammons, *The Art and Rhetoric of the Homeric Catalogue*).

As described by Sammons, there can be various strategies at work in even the most sparing lists. First of all, a catalog can be a way to introduce elements that do not otherwise fit into a narrative, or elements that do not necessarily need to be spelled out in detail or woven into the rest of the narrative. Though tangential to the main story, these types of elements can still take on added significance when grouped together in a catalog.

A catalog may also serve to establish a historical backdrop or mythic frame (i.e., to point out that historic figures or deities experienced similar situations), which is what Homer appears to be doing when he invokes the Muses in the first line of many of his catalogs. And, by invoking Muses or other mythic forces, the role of the storyteller temporarily shifts, becoming more "authoritative" by association, or slipping momentarily into the background.

The most powerful role of catalogs, however, is the way they can be used to put a spotlight on significant paradigms or models by listing many illuminating examples in succession. If you list some animals, for example, the reader will be challenged to think about what links these animals together and what paradigm they represent. And the power of a catalog lies in the fact that relationships between items are not explicitly spelled out, so readers must reach into their own memories and imaginations to arrive at unexpected destinations. The paradigm itself is merely hinted at through a drumbeat of repetitions that trigger readers to be on the lookout for underlying meanings.

Mainly used in the writing of many of the world's greatest epics, catalogs could also serve as tools in the writing of nature narratives. There are many aspects of the natural world that could be listed, and even ordinary things might point to something unique when they are organized in a list. How about a catalog of flower parts, or trees specific to a place, or items needed for a particular hike? What about the names of colors in a place, or descriptions of textures, or lists of local natural processes?

Keep in mind, however, that a catalog of items may or may not suggest something at that point in a narrative—a catalog may be given elevated meaning later in a story. What will the catalog signify? You get to decide.

"While she herself, as grain, brings up mankind on what is dry."
—Euripides, *The Bacchae*

RITUAL WORDS AND BILINGUAL TEXT

IN HIS FAR-REACHING EXPLORATIONS of myth, Joseph Campbell makes a very important point about ritual language. Ritual language, by definition, is unusual and looks strange because it is not part of conventional language (what Campbell calls the "language of domesticity"). Through familiarity and daily use, conventional words lose their ability to open up levels of deeper mystical experience—hence our need for powerful, unfamiliar ritual words.

Ritual words and ritual language do not (and do not have to) enter common speech, so they are free to follow their own rules and structures, which means they offer incredibly fertile terrain for language-making. This is an opportunity that every writer should be aware of because it is a place where the natural world, and our experiences in this world, can bubble up in utterly unique ways.

There is no limit to how far you can develop your own ritual words and ritual language, yet at the same time it is probably not realistic to write an entire piece using these unfamiliar forms. One alternative might be to instead write "bilingual text" by interspersing ritual words and ritual language at key moments in a text (akin to the poetic techniques of *prosimetrum* and *macaronic verse*).

Within a story, for instance, you could highlight extraordinary insights, make significant observations, or provide directions for ritual actions or utterances in a language that contrasts with your conventional storytelling voice. Imagine that these nuggets of language are like veins of ore in a rocky outcrop, or like acorns on the forest floor, or like current swirling beneath a river's placid surface—make them moments of condensed energy that rise up from a hidden world.

What this ritual language looks like will be up to you, but it might incorporate one or more concepts from this book, and it will probably utilize letters, sounds, rhythms, and word elements in new and provocative ways. It might repeat words and phrases, it might loop back into itself multiple times, and it might confuse your readers—but that is okay, because the purpose of ritual language is to break the rules of conventional language so that the worlds of raw nature, elemental powers, and mystical experiences can be mirrored in words.

If traditional or mythic knowledge is seen for its inaccuracies then our task must be to advance and refine that knowledge, not dismiss the entire body of knowledge as trivial or foolish.

Language beyond common comprehension
is a mystery,
a language of the gods.

RING COMPOSITION

biting the tail of the past

RING COMPOSITION is an enormously important, ancient storytelling technique that is largely absent from our modern "linear" world. This technique first arose in preliterate oral traditions but persisted in early written literatures because it almost certainly activated deep neurological pathways in our brains. In fact, the famed linguist Roman Jakobson described parallel, repeating correspondences, such as those found in ring compositions, as a key aspect of the primal relationship between language, grammar, and the brain.

Modern readers have been taught to dismiss such parallelisms as the mark of inept or lazy writers, but perceptive rereadings by a growing number of scholars are highlighting the degree to which ring compositions are the defining structures of countless narratives ranging from Homer's *Iliad* and the Bible (see Mary Douglas, *Thinking in Circles: An Essay in Ring Composition*) to Indo-European rituals and prayers (see Calvert Watkins, *How to Kill a Dragon*).

At their most basic level, ring compositions are circular narrative structures that finish where they begin (thus framing metaphorical journeys away from "home" and then back again). These rings are marked at their starting and ending points by the repeated use of key words or phrases, and the circular structure may be further accentuated through the repetition of distinctive cases, tenses, or rhetorical structures, or by other types of echoes. Rings usually occur in passages longer than a few sentences, but they can be built at the level of the phrase, sentence, stanza, paragraph, or text. It is even possible to loop many smaller rings together inside a single long ring.

Here are two brief examples. First an unadorned ring from Homer's *Odyssey*, which occurs when the hero returns home unexpectedly and is noticed first by his faithful dog (I have underlined the key ringing words for clarity):

> ... a <u>dog</u> who was <u>lying there</u> raised his head and ears. This was <u>Argos</u>, patient-hearted Odysseus' dog, whom he himself raised, but got no joy of him, since before that he went to sacred Ilion. In the days before, the young men had taken him out to follow goats of the wild, and deer, and rabbits; but now he had been put aside, with his master absent, and lay on the deep pile of dung, from the mules and oxen, which lay abundant before the gates, so that the servants of Odysseus could take it to his great estate, for manuring.
> <u>There</u> the <u>dog Argos lay</u>...."

(Book 17, lines 290–300 in the Lattimore translation)

And a highly elaborated ring in a speech by Achilles in Shakespeare's play *Troilus and Cressida* (III, iii. lines 103–11; with key phrases and echoes underlined). In particular, notice how the repeated *b* is visually mirrored ("eye to eye") by the repeated *d*.

> <u>This</u> <u>is</u> <u>not</u> <u>strange</u>, Ulysses.
> The <u>b</u>eauty that is <u>b</u>orne here in the face
> The bearer knows not, but commends itself
> To others' eyes; nor doth the eye itself,
> That most pure spirit of sense, behold itself,
> Not going from itself; <u>eye</u> <u>to</u> <u>eye</u> opposed,
> Salutes each other with each other's form;
> For speculation turns not to itself,
> Till it hath travell'<u>d</u> and is [mirror'<u>d</u>] there
> Where it may see itself. <u>This</u> <u>is</u> <u>not</u> <u>strange</u> at all.

While even simple rings will challenge readers who see only

tiresome repetition and overlook the deeper import, narrative-length rings are exceedingly complex—both for writers who must skillfully construct them and for readers who must tease out the underlying structures. Such is the case with Homer's *Iliad*, one of the most important pieces of literature ever written, which is built around a dazzlingly complex 1-9-1-12-8-12-1-9-1 ring (with the numbers referring to sequences of time within the story).

Mary Douglas observes that ring compositions in longer narratives follow predictable patterns. There is, first of all, a starting point that introduces the main characters and the dilemma to be faced through the use of key words and word phrases. The ensuing narrative is then constructed as a journey "out" to a crucial midpoint (the turn) and then "back" home to the starting point. Vital to this construction is the repeated use of the same key words or phrases at the beginning, midpoint, and conclusion. It is also essential that the journey "out" is divided into a series of well-marked episodes that develop the trajectory of the story's main theme, and that the journey after the midpoint inverts this sequence to form a second series of exactly matched episodes on the way back "home" (**A**-B-C-**D**-C´-B´-**A**´).

To a modern reader these matched sections will feel like unnecessary repetition, but they work by setting up the parallels (correspondences) which Jakobson describes as the core activity that exists between the brain and language. In the hands of a skilled writer these analogies reveal deep and unexpected layers of meaning not apparent until the reader is prompted by the matched pairs to look more closely at the text. Ring compositions may even be thought of as ecosystems of language because, unlike ordinary sentence structures (with nouns and verbs arranged in simple relationships like predators and prey), ring compositions set up multitiered ecologies of complex meaning.

All this may seem academic unless the modern writer takes the time to learn how to tap into and utilize the power of this ancient storytelling technique. Because rings are so difficult to construct and to perceive, they have been used since antiquity to mark, set aside, or elevate the language of discrete passages—a way of saying "this is important, pay attention here." Rings were often used in victory, funeral, or celebratory texts, and they were very important in the ritual language of chants, prayers, and poems.

In the same way they could be used to re-create a ritual language that is otherwise missing from modern literature. Nature writers might also consider weaving in some of the ring cycles found in nature such as the seasons, equinoxes and solstices, the passage of the sun and moon, hydrologic cycles, or food chains. However they are constructed, rings will be most powerful when they build little nests of sacred meaning that can be used to measure our lives. It will be up to each writer to learn how to harness this tool that is as old as storytelling itself.

We all follow the same neural pathways
in pursuit of our gods.

RITUAL CHANTING

CHANTS ARE MONOTONOUS, rhythmic utterances that fall somewhere between regular speech and singing. They can be incredibly complex in structure and uttered over many days by highly trained performers, or they can be as simple as a high school riff on "GO TEAM GO!"

Chants (also called "speech-songs") are distinguished by their use of alliteration, rhythmic sound, formulas, and nonsense syllables to create compelling sound environments that carry the symbolic knowledge of a self-defined group of people. Chants are one of language's most powerful tools because they bring people together and unite them in temporary societies organized around the rhythmic structures of monotonously repeated sounds.

Because of this, chants are best thought of as ceremonies or ritual acts that create sacred spaces and convey sacred knowledge. This is how chants have been used in all known cultures as far back as their histories can be reconstructed, and this is why chants show up in an immense variety of hymns, spells, incantations, prayers, invocations, mantras, and sutras. For example, the earliest known Hittite chant from the sixteenth century BC includes the lines:

> Clothes of Nesa, clothes of Nesa—approach me, approach!
> Bring me to my mother—approach me, approach!
> Bring me to my *uwa*—approach me, approach!

Another example from around the same time is an Akkadian hymn to Ishtar that reads in part:

> Praise the goddess, the most awesome of goddesses.
> Let us revere the mistress of the people, the greatest of the [gods].
> Praise Ishtar, the most awesome of the goddesses.
> Let us revere the queen of women, the greatest of the [gods].
> (both examples from Pritchard, *The Ancient Near East*)

The logical mind balks at these repetitive phrases—impatient perhaps for a narrative thread, a plot, or a little variety—but that is exactly the purpose of chants, especially ritual chants. They are meant to serve the music of the heart rather than the mind; they are meant to immerse you and hold you inside rhythmic sound for the sake of the sound itself, in a transcendent space where no other meaning is required.

A historical emphasis on religious symbols and deities makes us overlook the fact that chants could be composed of nature words and images as well. In fact, anyone who acknowledges or celebrates the natural world could use ritual chanting as one way to express the deeper states of knowledge that arise from this awareness.

Chants must also be embedded in a rich cultural or spiritual context or the words lose all meaning save for their inherent beauty. Sadly, modern society has for the most part lost many of these contexts, so the best we can do is fumble hopefully toward them. This will result in some silly sounding early efforts, but the *intent* of moving toward ritual chanting is what matters.

Maybe we could try writing something along the lines of raga-like invocations for the sunrise, for the seasons, or for birds, all with an ear toward creating emotional ribbons of sound that might endure over time. I live in the mountains, so a ritual chant for my place could start off *mountain, mountain, mountain*. The shape of the landscape could be layered in with *mountain high, mountain low, mountain high, mountain low*. I could add some nonsense syllables such as *mountain ho-high, mountain la-low* and then accentuate the alliteration with *mountain ho-high higher mountain, mountain la-low lofty mountain*. Again, these are frivolous examples that lack a larger context, but it is the imperative of experimentation to start somewhere, and it is the work of writers to create narratives where their chants can find a home.

Look again at the chants from the sixteenth century BC (or at any old chants for that matter) and notice that they convey little to no emotional or spiritual significance for a modern reader. This is characteristic of chants: they are meant to carry meaning for a specific community of users, and outside this context they are reduced to mere words.

It's okay if a ritual chant sounds silly, mundane, or monotonous to other users. A chant's power stems from the way it works within a single community or, in the case of a writer, within a single narrative. And one day, maybe some writer will find a way to use chants as part of a thread that runs throughout an entire life's work.

❧

The only true eloquence is that spoken of home, heart, and freedom.

❧

RAVEN

kar 'loud noise'
> *kor*
>> corvus
>
> *kr*
>> raven
>> retch
>> ring
>
> *krep*
>> crack
>> creak
>> crevice
>
> *kri*
>> cricket

skr

    scream

    screech

    shrike

gar 'to cry hoarsely'

    crane

    croon

    crow

    garrulous

    grackle

ru 'to shout, yell'

    raucous

    rumor

⁍

SOUNDS

LANGUAGES ARE BUILT from units of sound, and sound is the first aspect of language we encounter. Long before we reach the age where we begin to read and write, we have already mastered the skills of speaking and listening to our language, and our remarkable capacity to shape sound and assign meaning to units of sound—even when they occur in an infinite variety of unique combinations—is one of our greatest human traits.

Speech sounds are a fascinating topic. A detailed survey lies outside the scope of this book, but a brief sketch of sound production might still be useful because language-making processes can succeed only to the extent that they produce harmonious sounds that people find pleasing and continue to use. It would be tiresome, for instance, to read, pronounce, or listen to a long series of words with harsh, contrasting sounds.

Words are built from syllables, and syllables are constructed from vowel cores that are capped by consonants at the beginning (*onset*) and/or end (*coda*) of each syllable. Harmonious patterns and rhymes are created as vowel cores, consonant onsets, consonant codas, syllables, and words work together to form the music of well-crafted language.

Take the word *constructed*, for instance. Each syllable, *con-struc-ted*, contains a vowel core (*o, u, e*), a consonant onset (*c, str, t*), and a consonant coda (*n, c, d*). These syllables are strongly marked with stop consonants that obstruct and then release the flow of air, making this a pleasingly rhythmic word to pronounce. The first syllable starts with a strong *k* sound then ends on a gliding *n* sound that flows perfectly into the sibilant *s* sound at the onset of the next syllable. The second syllable starts softly with the *s*, then has a pair of strong stops on the *t* and *k* sounds, while the third syllable satisfyingly closes the word with two more strong stops: *t* and *d*. At the same time, the sequence of vowel cores starts in the back of the mouth with *o* and *u* then sweeps forward into a high *e* in the front of the mouth for a final flourish.

It takes a lot of work to analyze the sounds of a single word like this, but having or developing a keen ear for these kinds of sound patterns is something that distinguishes great writers and will help anyone create new words. As with music, the sound of speech is most beautiful when it is corralled and shaped into pleasing patterns. With language the task is to move sound around the mouth in ways that produce these patterns: front to back; high to low; lips, tongue, palate, and throat all working together. This is the orchestra and you are the conductor.

Know Your Instrument: Vowels

Vowels are open sounds produced by vibrations of the vocal cords. You can feel these vibrations in your throat if you pronounce a long series of vowels such as *eeeeeeeeeeeeeeee*. Vowels are called "open" because they are produced in an open mouth rather than by obstructions of airflow (which are features of consonants). All vowels are marked by their quantity as well as their quality. Quantity is a measure of length: either short or long (compare the short *a* sound of *man* versus the long *a* sound of *mane*). Quality reflects the location of the vowel sound in the mouth cavity as determined by the position of the tongue and the rounding of the lips. Vowels produced in the back of the mouth, mainly the *o* and *u* sounds, are rounded because they require a rounding of the lips; other vowels are unrounded.

Vowels are an especially problematic aspect of the English sound system because the five vowel letters in our alphabet do not adequately map the twenty or so vowel sounds we use when speaking. This glaring discrepancy forces awkward solutions where single vowels end up representing a range of sounds (for instance, there are eight different *a* sounds in words like *rat, Kate, balm, any, about, mare, all, was*) or situations where a single sound is expressed by different vowel combinations. Consider how the same sound in *all, sauce, caught, talk, law, long, brought* is represented by *a, au, augh, al, aw, o, ough*, or how the same sound in *fate, pain, straight, pay, gauge, vein, they, feign, eight, great* is represented by *a, ai, aigh, ay, au, ei, ey, eig, eigh, ea* (examples from Emerson, *The History of the English Language*).

English clearly needs some new vowels, but for the time being it is worth learning the twelve pure vowel sounds and their features (there are also eight diphthongs, which are double vowels that complexly combine pure vowel sounds). Pure vowels are shaped by the tongue and produced in the front or back of the mouth, high or low in the mouth, or somewhere in between. Notice in the following list that we are speaking of vowels not as letters in the alphabet but as sounds that can be represented by different letter combinations. There are different conventions for writing these vowel sounds, so I have given two versions plus sample words to demonstrate each sound.

Front Vowels

i (also written as *ē*): *b<u>ee</u>, s<u>ea</u>, am<u>oe</u>ba*. Long *e* is a **high front vowel** produced high in the mouth and as far forward as possible; any higher or further forward and the sound would be a consonant.

ɪ (also *ĭ*): *b<u>i</u>t, h<u>i</u>m, hors<u>e</u>s*. Short *i* is also a **high front vowel**, but with tongue and jaw slightly lowered.

e (also *ā*): *b<u>ai</u>t, <u>a</u>pe, w<u>ai</u>st*. Long *a* is a **mid front vowel**, slightly lower than above.

ɛ (also *ĕ*): *l<u>eo</u>pard, d<u>ea</u>d, s<u>ai</u>d*. Short *e* is also a **mid front vowel**, but slightly lower than above.

æ (also *ă*): *h<u>a</u>nd, s<u>a</u>lmon, s<u>a</u>t*. Short *a* is a **low front vowel**, produced at the lowest point possible in the front of the mouth.

Center Vowels

ə (also *ɨ*): *sof<u>a</u>, <u>a</u>bout, moun<u>tai</u>n*. The schwa is a **mid center vowel** whose exact sound can be influenced by adjacent consonants; for example, next to an *r* the schwa can be "r-colored," as in words like *b<u>ir</u>d, h<u>er</u>d, f<u>ur</u>*.

ʌ (also *ɨ*): *s<u>u</u>n, <u>o</u>ven, fl<u>oo</u>d*. This is a **low center vowel**, though its position and sound has been described differently by various experts, and some put it in the back of the mouth.

Back Vowels

u (also *ū*): *soup, boot, sewer*. Long *u* is a **high back vowel**, produced high in the mouth like *i* but shifted as far back as possible.

ʋ (also *ŭ*): *foot, bull, wolf*. Short *u* is a **high back vowel**, but with tongue and jaw slightly lowered.

o (also *ō*): *boat, toe, toad*. Long *o* is a **mid back vowel**.

ɔ (also *ŏ*): *stalk, author, saw*. Short *o* is a **mid back vowel**, slightly lower than above.

a (also *a*): *father, calm, tar*. This is a **low back vowel**, produced as low and as far back as possible.

The rising and falling sequences of vowel sounds in successive syllables help shape the music of language, and these patterns, occurring in both expected and unexpected combinations, make language endlessly fascinating. Few people realize that for thousands of years there have been countless small adjustments in the lengths, pitches, and sounds of different vowel combinations in order to match the changing tastes of each historical period. For example, speakers at the tail end of the Old English period began shortening long vowel sounds when additional consonants or syllables were added to the ends of words, giving us pairs like *sheep-shepherd* (long *ē* → short *ě*), *Christ-Christmas* (long *ī* → short *ĭ*; long *ī* is actually the dipthong *ai*), *bone-bonfire* (long *ō* → short *ŏ*). Notice in this example that there's no reason why the vowel sounds need to be shortened; we could just as easily pronounce the longer words with the longer vowel sounds, but the shortened sounds are a historical convention that we continue to use.

One way to learn how to harness the language-making power of vowel sounds is to play with the ways they feel and sound in the mouth. Consider the random sequence *it-her-you* and notice how the vowel sounds (*i, e, ou*) shift in your mouth from front to back. Now add *falls* to the list and notice that the sequence sinks to the bottom of your mouth under the dead weight of the low back vowel. This sequence would be a dud, but if you add *for it* at the end you discover that the collapsing sequence suddenly springs out of your mouth with a strong rising close: *it-her-you-falls-for-it* (feel the sounds of the vowels in your mouth as you carefully pronounce this sequence). Always be conscious of the movement of vowel sounds in your mouth, because a lively, varying cadence and rhythm of vowels will bring your words to life.

Know Your Instrument: Consonants

In a way consonants are more straightforward than vowels because the twenty-one consonant letters in English closely map the twenty-four consonant sounds we use, but they are also more complicated because the production of consonant sounds involves bundles of articulatory processes. Consonants differ from vowels (open sounds) because they are produced by the blocking or partial blocking of airflow, and they can be further voiced or unvoiced by vibrating or not vibrating the vocal cords (compare the vibrating voiced *z* of *z-z-z-z-zebra* against the soft voiceless *s* of *s-s-s-s-snake*).

Consonants are not always easy to classify, and the quality of a consonant sound may shift depending on the letters that precede or follow it, but in general, consonants can be categorized in two ways: by the location in the mouth where they are produced and by the manner in which they are produced.

Locations Are Named as Follows:

Labial These consonants are produced by bringing the two lips together (bilabials) *p, b, m,* and *w,* or by bringing the upper teeth against the lower lip (labiodentals) *f* and *v.* Of these, *b, m, v,* and *w* are voiced, while *p* and *f* are voiceless. Try saying each letter out loud to hear these sounds.

213

Dental Produced with the tip of the tongue between the teeth or against the upper teeth, ð (voiced as in _then_) and θ (voiceless as in _thin_).

Alveolar Produced with the front of the tongue against the raised ridge behind the front teeth, _t, d, n, s, z_, and _l_. Of these, _d, n, z_, and _l_ are voiced; _t_ and _s_ are voiceless.

Palatal Produced with the blade of the tongue against the hard roof of the mouth, ž (voiced as in _measure_), š (voiceless as in _sure_), ǰ (voiced as in _gem_), and č (voiceless as in _nature_).

Velar Produced with the back of the tongue pressed against the soft roof of the mouth, _k, g_, ŋ (as in _sing_), and _w_. Of these, _g_, ŋ, and _w_ are voiced, while _k_ is voiceless.

The manner of articulation (the ways in which consonant sounds are produced) is a complicated concept, but we can begin by distinguishing between sounds produced with a full stoppage of the airflow (_stops_) versus sounds produced by a partial escape of air (_continuants_). The latter group can be further divided into sounds produced when we constrict airflow to create audible friction (_fricatives_), sounds produced by a brief stop followed by a release of air (_affricates_), and sounds produced by air escaping through the nose rather than the mouth (_nasals_). Again, all of these sounds may be voiced or voiceless.

Stops These consonants are produced when airflow is fully blocked by the lips (_p, b_, and _m_), tongue against teeth (_t, d_, and _n_), or tongue against the soft roof of the mouth (_k, g_, and ŋ). Some authorities also classify the nasals (_m, n_, and ŋ) as stops because the production of these sounds involves blocking air in the mouth even though it is allowed to escape through the nasal cavity.

Fricatives Produced by an audible release of air through a constricted part of the mouth, including the lips (_f_ and _v_), teeth (*θ* and *ð*), or tongue (*s*, *š*, *z*, and *ž*).

Affricates Produced by a brief blockage against the roof of the mouth followed by a release of air (*č* and *ǰ*).

I mentioned earlier that consonants are bundles of articulatory processes, which means that each consonant sound is a combination of the features described above. Now that some of the essential terminology has been presented we can describe each consonant in turn.

p is a **voiceless labial stop**; as in *a<u>pp</u>le, <u>p</u>eak, <u>p</u>ear.*

b is a **voiced labial stop**; *<u>b</u>at, <u>b</u>ear, <u>b</u>lack.*

m is a **voiced labial nasal**; *<u>m</u>arsh, <u>m</u>oss, <u>m</u>ountain.*

t is a **voiceless alveolar stop**; *<u>t</u>ern, <u>t</u>ick, <u>t</u>omca<u>t</u>.*

d is a **voiced alveolar stop**; *<u>d</u>andelion, <u>d</u>og, <u>d</u>onkey.*

n is a **voiced alveolar nasal**; *s<u>n</u>ow, <u>n</u>ature, <u>n</u>ight.*

k is a **voiceless velar stop**; *<u>c</u>at, o<u>ch</u>er, tur<u>k</u>ey.*

g is a **voiced velar stop**; *<u>g</u>uard, <u>gh</u>ost, <u>g</u>a<u>g</u>.*

ŋ is a **voiced velar nasal**; *fi<u>ng</u>er, a<u>ng</u>le, lo<u>ng</u>.*

f is a **voiceless labial fricative**; *<u>f</u>ish, ree<u>f</u>, cou<u>gh</u>, <u>ph</u>oebe.*

v is a **voiced labial fricative**; *do<u>v</u>e, <u>v</u>ast, <u>v</u>al<u>v</u>e.*

s is a **voiceless alveolar fricative**; *<u>s</u>ap, <u>s</u>nake, <u>c</u>ereal.*

z is a **voiced alveolar fricative**; *<u>z</u>oo, pea<u>s</u>, kangroo<u>s</u>.*

θ is a **voiceless dental fricative**; *<u>th</u>igh, <u>th</u>istle, mo<u>th</u>, tee<u>th</u>.*

ð is a **voiced dental fricative**; *mo<u>th</u>er, <u>th</u>en, ei<u>th</u>er, tee<u>the</u>.*

š is a **voiceless palatal fricative**; *mar<u>sh</u>, fi<u>sh</u>, gla<u>ci</u>al, <u>sh</u>ell, <u>s</u>ugar.*

ž is a **voiced palatal fricative**; *a<u>z</u>ure, ca<u>s</u>ualty, vi<u>si</u>on.*

č is a **voiceless palatal affricate**; *<u>ch</u>urch, mat<u>ch</u>, righ<u>te</u>ous, na<u>t</u>ure.*

ǰ is a **voiced palatal affricate**; *<u>j</u>elly, re<u>gi</u>on, resi<u>d</u>ual, ju<u>dge</u>.*

l is a **voiced alveolar continuant** (sometimes called a "liquid" because it is produced with some constriction in the mouth but not enough to be a fricative); *l̲eaf, pl̲ant, pul̲p, singl̲e.*

r is a **voiced continuant** (or liquid); *r̲eef, r̲ock, car̲p, r̲eptile.*

w is a **voiced labial and velar semivowel** (sometimes called a "glide" because it is produced with no constriction in the mouth); *qu̲een, w̲itch, w̲atch, sw̲im.*

y is a **voiced palatal semivowel** (or glide); *bay̲, y̲es, y̲ou.*

h is a **voiceless glottal** ("in the throat") **glide or fricative**; *h̲ole, h̲ash, h̲at, w̲ho.*

You would have to work pretty hard to learn all this terminology and study sounds with this degree of precision, but the reward can be an ever-growing command of the pacing, rhythm, and orchestrated movement of sound in your writing. This understanding is also critical to the language-making process, especially if you are creating new words by removing, swapping, or shifting letters, because letter shifts often occur within the same articulatory groups (what the *Princeton Encyclopedia of Poetry and Poetics* calls "equivalence sets"). For instance, the process of transforming the ancient Latin word *pater* into the Modern English word *father* involved a switch of labial *p* to labial *f*. In this case both *p* and *f* are voiceless, but many words in English have been created simply by swapping voiceless and voiced letters from the same articulatory group. Examples include *fi̲ne/vi̲ne, seal̲/zeal̲, rich̲/ridg̲e, wreath̲/wreath̲e.* Another common swap is between consonants formed in the mouth (orals) versus the nose (nasals); for example, *rib̲/rim̲, dig̲/ding̲, mad̲/man̲.* All the articulatory groups offer examples like this, pointing to the many ways that sound patterns have profoundly influenced language-making processes.

*Go beyond ordinary words like "diving" and seek out utterly
unexpected words like "whalesgoingdeep" that make people
stop and think, and talk amongst one another.*

PAUSE AND EFFECT

AS A MATTER of course, and almost without being conscious
of the fact, we use conventional punctuation symbols to shape
our writing. From an early age we are taught to follow rules
and suggestions for the use of periods, commas, dashes, parentheses, and other marks, and we are shown how the proper application of punctuation helps guide readers and shape
meaning.

What many people do not realize is that punctuation is
a fairly recent invention that marked a profound shift from
ancient oral cultures, in which words were spoken out loud,
to modern cultures, in which printed words are read in silence (see *Pause and Effect: An Introduction to the History of
Punctuation in the West* by M. B. Parkes). The original impetus
for this shift seems to have grown out of the need to radically
unify and disseminate Christian doctrine in the sixth century,
yet punctuation is now so well established that it has become
an unquestioned feature of modern culture.

Prior to the invention of punctuation, ancient texts were
written in *scriptio continua*, with letters and words strung together continuously with no spaces or marks. It seems as
though this would be confusing, but *scriptio continua* has a

217

profound advantage because it forces readers to speak a text out loud and arrive at meaning by actively grappling with one word at a time. The result is a much deeper engagement with text as well as highly personal interpretations of meaning by each reader (exactly what the Church was trying to prevent).

When approaching punctuation it is worth keeping two things in mind: punctuation is a relatively recent invention and is therefore only one way of thinking about text, and punctuation is nothing more than a box of codified behaviors promoted by a dominant mainstream culture. It may or may not serve you to follow the rules of punctuation, but it is still important to consider this question carefully and to think about your choices.

Why not play around and see if something else is a better fit for you? There is a huge range of rarely used symbols available. You might try the technique offered by Boncompagno da Signa (ca. 1165–1240), who used only an upright virgule / to mark pauses where the sense was not complete and a level virgule – where the sense was complete. Or you might experiment with different structural approaches like highlighting the thesis or boundaries of each paragraph with unique symbols, or you might devise new ways to highlight questions versus declarations through the structure of a sentence rather than with punctuation.

Better yet, why not look to nature for the types of punctuation it offers? What are the seasons, for instance, if not bundles of punctuation marks on the seamless narrative of the year? As you wander in the natural world, what are the edges of a meadow, the lines of a river, the ripples of clouds, or the upright forms of trees if not ways of marking (punctuating) your passage through the time and space of a story?

In fact, we live in a world of punctuation: not as marks on a page but as vivid objects and moments that we can inhabit and turn our awareness to. What does it feel like to be in this landscape of natural punctuation? What is it like to stop inside a period and really contemplate this place? It is right there, in the world around you; go find it and tell us what it feels like. Pause with a comma, run with a dash, or uncover hidden parentheses, but give them the shape of nature.

Punctuation Play

Try Boncompagno's model using only two types of punctuation:

> I could speak of the animals I saw today / or I could speak of meaning – One is a list of sorts / the other a sort of list – Both are a compilation held together with string – Here in my cabin I hang them from the walls like bundles of drying herbs / or carefully tended hunting utensils – They are reminder / or tool / shaping my writing when I glance up –

Or try this with *scriptio continua*, while spacing out key words:

> Icouldspeakofthe animals Isawtoday / orIcould speak ofmeaning – Oneisa list ofsorts / theotherasortoflist – Botharea compilation heldtogetherwithstring – HereinmycabinIcanhangthemfromthewallslike bundles ofdryingherbs / orcarefully tended huntingutensils – Theyarereminderor / tool / shapingmy writing whenIglanceup –

Or try replacing punctuation with phrases that imply the punctuation, perhaps in combination with *scriptio continua* (here I am naming the implied punctuation with square brackets for the purpose of demonstration):

> Iamrunningdownthehillsidetotheriver steppingoveralog [comma] jumpingwildlyandlovingeveryminuteofit sunbeamontheground[period] Mygoalistoswiminthewater itissuchahotday[period] Finallythereitis[comma] Iamstandingontheriverbank strippingoffmyclothes[comma] foralongdeliciousplungeinthewater[period]

Maybe it would work to come up with a convention to set off these punctuation phrases:

> Iamrunningdownthehillsidetotheriver <<steppingoveralog>>
> jumpingwildlyandlovingeveryminuteofit
> <<sunbeamontheground>> ...

Or space the main text while leaving punctuation phrases in *scriptio continua*:

> I am running down the hillside to the river steppingoveralog
> jumping wildly and loving every minute of it
> sunbeamontheground Finally ...

Another idea might be to imitate the style of old "punctuation poems," in which a poem reveals two readings depending on which set of punctuation you follow. Here is a well-known example of a punctuation poem from the late Middle Ages that gives two different readings of the clergy's motivations depending on whether you take out the virgules and punctuate the poem with the periods or take out the periods and punctuate the poem with the virgules:

> Trusty. seldom / to their friends unjust. /
> Glad for to help. no Christian creature /
> willing to grieve. setting all their joy and lust
> only in the pleasure / of God. having no care /
> who is most rich. with them they will be sure /
> where need is. giving neither reward nor fee /
> unreasonably. thus live priests. in the name of God. /

The point in all these exercises is to experiment fearlessly with breaking conventional thinking about punctuation, and these are just a few examples of how unexpected the results can look. Most of these experiments will not be useful, but you might just stumble upon a new style or a new way of thinking about writing that appeals to you.

❧

SPACING OUT

play with syl la bles and un ex pec ted let ter choiyzs as one way to
fo cus onthewordasa tan gi ble li ving en tit y rat her than on
nar ra tive mean ing or li ter ar y con struc tion

WHEN I STARTED READING Paul Saenger's book *Space Between Words: The Origins of Silent Reading*, I assumed that this was an obscure and tangential topic. It came as a shock to discover that the study of spaces between words is profoundly important and that the body of literature on the topic is so immense that Saenger's 480-page book includes 130 pages of reference matter.

We tend to take the spaces between words (along with our expectation that each word has to have known boundaries) for granted, on the idea that this is the only reasonable way to read and interpret text. However, as I mentioned in the previous section, nearly all texts prior to the seventh century were written in *scriptio continua* (also called *scriptura continua*), in which words and sentences were strung together continuously with no spaces. Even after spaces were introduced in the seventh and eighth centuries, it took another 500 years before the practice of using spaces to separate words became widespread and readily accepted in Europe.

It might seem that endless strings of letters would look absurd to a modern reader, yet researchers have found that children have no problem reading *scriptio continua* until about fifth grade, at which point a child begins to struggle with the expectation that there should be spaces. Studies such as these demonstrate that the reading of spaced text is a learned rather than innate ability.

Researchers are intrigued by these discoveries because it turns out that the ways that words and letters are spaced have significant effects on our cognitive neurophysiology. Studying the ways that people read and perceive different texts is helping scientists understand how the brain works and why people with learning impairments or cognitive damage sometimes struggle to read.

In fact, the introduction of spaces between words signals one of the most significant cultural shifts in human history. In antiquity, a text written in *scriptio continua* had to be read slowly and out loud, usually together with other people, as the reader methodically broke strings of letters into meaningful units. Because there were few conventional word orders or word definitions at that time, readers would hold clusters of letters in their minds until they reached the end of a passage and then double back to start thinking about how the clusters might fit together to form grammar and meaning.

This sounds laborious, and probably was, but it is important to realize that trying to read a text rapidly was not a goal of readers in antiquity. Many texts were meant to be savored and interpreted continually and fruitfully over one's lifetime.

As one small concession, vowels were eventually introduced as a way to help mark syllable boundaries, but it was not until much later that word boundaries were formalized with physical spaces. Then, for the first time, the presence of spaces and the isolation of repeatable groups of letters began to create a sense that each word was a unique "sign." Readers could then begin to recognize and memorize "word silhouettes"—the clear outlines and conventional boundaries of each word (what is known as a word's *Bouma shape*).

Along with the steadily growing memorization of word

silhouettes, very short words and articles (e.g., *the, a, an*) were introduced from the vernacular speech of common people, further relieving the tedium of reading long polysyllabic texts. All these factors conspired to gradually shift the process of reading from an act of extended interpretation to an activity that consisted of memorization and rapid consumption.

What happens in terms of cognitive neurophysiology is that a reader sees and experiences something very different on the page when text is broken up with spaces and short words. Specifically, the introduction of spaces greatly expands a reader's *parafoveal vision*—the unfocused span of text (usually fifteen to twenty letters in width) that a reader unconsciously perceives on each side of the text that is being clearly observed and read in the zone of *foveal vision* (straight ahead). As a result a modern reader can simply glance at text (whether in large blocks or in short, catchy slogans), and by instantly recognizing a span of word silhouettes and word boundaries rather than studying each letter, the reader can "read" very rapidly without consciously scanning every single letter and word.

One consequence of this shift is that reading has become an internalized and silent activity, what specialists call "silent reading." This is a fantastic development if you want to create a fast-moving consumer culture in which information is rapidly and efficiently processed, but it is worth asking what happens to a society, to a culture, and to a democracy when the act of reading shifts from a collective, oral experience to an isolated, silent experience. It may be that silent reading helped lead to the blossoming of the individual (which many people seem to hold as a positive value), but isolated individuals are also easier to control, and they lose the ethical grounding of the communal dialogue.

Word-Spacing Practice

A lot changes if you start experimenting with removing

spaces between words, but I want to focus on one particular aspect: it dramatically shrinks a reader's parafoveal vision and forces the reader to slow down, profoundly transforming the entire experience of engaging with and thinking about text. A careful writer who understands this concept might be able to remove spaces as a strategy that opens up new realms of awareness or startles readers out of a consumer mindset in which objects and ideas are easily consumed and disposed of.

The reality is that modern readers no longer have the patience or willingness to digest large blocks of *scriptio continua* (although we don't think twice about using *scriptio continua* on a daily basis when we write email and internet addresses), but a writer might still use this technique in other skillful ways. For instance, short stretches of *scriptio continua* could be used to insert elevated or ritual language in the midst of a much longer narrative. Or short bits could be run together to form unique phrases for speaking directly about the natural world (e.g., *blackbearhome, salmonriverrunning*).

Throughout the history of written language there have been many fascinating conventions for spacing text, and there is room for many more experiments. There have been times when symbols were used instead of spaces, thus mimicking the neurophysiological effects of *scriptio continua* but with an open look that might be more inviting to a modern reader (the·interpunct, a·midlevel·dot, was·one·popular·symbol·used· during·the·early·Middle·Ages). And although ancient Greeks wrote in *scriptio continua* they sometimes inserted spaces between the letters of a specific word that was under discussion (whatwedonowwhenweput q u o t a t i o n m a r k s aroundaword). For a period of time, writers using *scriptio continua* would capitalize the last letter of meaningful phrases in order to create a sense of boundaries (the opposite of our modern practice of capitalizing the first letter of a sentencE).

Space could also be used in other inventive ways. How

about inserting a space between every syllable and taking out all punctuation and capitalization? Or inserting a space between every syllable and then using bits of *scriptio continua* to mark the ends of each distinct idea (with no other punctuation)? Or writing in *scriptio continua* but with occasional spaces inserted to create unexpected breaks?

Keep in mind that altering the spaces between words is like playing with fire because these changes affect the cognitive neurophysiology of your readers. This is a power to be respectful of, and the intent should not be to bewilder or lead readers astray. A writer should always lean toward clarity, aesthetic harmony, and deeper meaning through these experiments. This will be the intention that leads to changes that might endure and help shape culture.

❦

singagainsongrollaroundsongdownthewindsong
blessedsongwearefreeaslongassoundissongsong

❦

METATHESIS

LANGUAGE HAS A NIFTY trick up its sleeve, and that is its ability (and willingness) to switch around adjacent letters to create new words. Modern English speakers might never think to swap letters in the word *wasp* to form the word *waps*, yet these two words were used interchangeably in Middle English for over a hundred years. And if you keep digging, you will find many, many other examples of words with switched letters stretching all the way from ancient languages that predated Old English right up to the present day. The fact that we count to the number *three* but divide something into *thirds* is a relic of letter switching from Old English, while our mispronunciation of *pretty* as *purty* is an example of active switching in Modern English.

Formally called *metathesis*, this process of rearranging or switching adjacent letters, sounds, or syllables is sometimes dismissed by linguists as trivial pronunciation ("performance") errors or child's play (children often switch letters around), but it is clear that metathesis is a regular and highly productive process of word formation in all the world's languages.

No unified theory exists to explain metathesis, but in some cases it seems to result from the conscious or unconscious shifting of sounds or syllables to simplify language for speakers who stumble over the "proper" forms of words. Consider a few illustrative examples from Modern English: perfectly legitimate words such as *cavalry, comfortable, integral, introduce,* and *prescription* are increasingly spoken as *calvary, comfterble, intergal, interduce,* and *perscription* (often to the point where speakers become confused about which form is correct). Over time, some or all of these "mispronounced" words may end up encoded in alternate spellings that more accurately reflect everyday speech. Spellings like *introduce* and *interduce* could potentially exist side by side, as *wasp* and *waps* did in Middle English, for long periods of time until one form takes clear precedence. Or two forms can continue to exist side by side with the same meaning, as in our word *ne<u>rv</u>e* alongside the combining form *ne<u>ur</u>o-* (notice that *v* and *u* were historically the same letter).

Metathesis may also create changes that seem (at least from a distance) even more bizarre and unexpected. For example,

Old English *brid* is now our *bird*, and Old Norse *hross* is now our *horse*. And there is a large group of words that started *hw* in Old English that now start *wh* in Modern English, including such common words as *what, where, when, whale, wheat,* and *white*. It hardly makes sense that *hwael* became our *whale*, but that is the magic of metathesis.

Metathesis typically works to corral the wayward tentacles of a language and bring awkwardly pronounced words into conformity with the traditional sound patterns of that language (for example, see Chomsky and Halle's *Sound Pattern of English*), but metathesis may also open the door for experimentation and the development of colloquial speech or local dialects. This kind of experimentation seems to be where the real fun happens, and it is an open invitation for your own writing.

Be on the lookout for opportunities to practice metathesis with any of the words you use to describe the natural world. Here is a fascinating place to play with sounds or craft unexpected puns between sound and meaning. Try crazy things like changing *dragonfly* into *dar-gon-fly*, and don't worry if this sounds totally stupid at first. Many such experiments will be duds, but somewhere out there are little gems that will change our language forever.

᪥

Lewis Thomas on word roots:
"When you run across a primary, original word,
the experience is both disturbing and vaguely pleasurable."

᪥

SHIFTY LETTERS

ONE OF THE primary ways that languages change over time is when individual letters are replaced by other letters. A classic example can be seen in the transformation of the older *p* of Latin to the newer *f* of the Germanic languages, as in Latin *pater* versus English *father*. Letter shifts often follow changes in pronunciation, but phonology (the study of sounds in language) is a very complex topic, so let us focus on what we see on the page, the written forms of letters, and not worry here about underlying sound patterns.

At the same time it is helpful to recognize that when letters change they are most often replaced by other letters from the same articulatory group because these shifts are easier to make. For instance, a labial consonant (one spoken with the lips) is more likely to shift to another labial consonant (*p* and *f* are both labial consonants). Therefore, one way to understand letter shifts is to divide them into groups such as *labial, dental* (sounds made with the tip of the tongue against your teeth), *palatal* (sounds made with tongue pressed against the roof of your mouth), or *velar* (sounds made in the back of your throat).

Another way to understand letter shifts is to group them into historical periods or languages of origin, although these groupings might change depending on how far back you go. For instance, if you compare Latin *fiber* against English *beaver*, you can point to two letter shifts, *f→b* (*fiber*/*beaver*) and *b→v* (*fiber*/*beaver*), but if you compare the more recent Old English *beofor* to English *beaver*, then you get an example of a different letter shift, *f→v* (*beofor*/*beaver*).

Here is a simple alphabetic list of some letter shifts, along with a few examples of how they have affected English as we use it today. Some of these letter shifts look abrupt (e.g., *fiber* → *beaver*) because they involve intermediate steps that have been left out in the interest of space. I am here more interested in the letter shift itself than in tracing the history of each shift, but anyone with a deeper interest can pursue these shifts in greater detail with *The Oxford English Dictionary* or other sources.

My intent is to shed light on a diversity of letter shifts in English, and this is not a complete list, nor is it conclusive. It is also important to understand that letter shifts are not one-way streets, nor are they endpoints. Any letter that has already shifted could shift again in a new direction or even revert to an earlier form (in fact many letters have already shifted multiple times). For example, *whale* could return to something like its original Old English spelling *hwale* (which is more phonetically accurate anyway), or *ring* could revert to its Old English spelling *hring* (notice that *h-ring* has a nicer sound too). Other letters that have not already shifted could shift in the future with some of these patterns in mind.

a → o/oa: Latin *mater* → English *mother*; Old English *ac* → English *oak*, *ban* → *bone*, *bat* → *boat*, *fam* → *foam*, *pal* → *pole*, *rad* → *road*, *stan* → *stone*

ae → ea/ee: Old English *daed* → English *deed*, *haete* → *heat*, *hwaete* → *wheat*, *sae* → *sea*, *saed* → *seed*, *slaepan* → *sleep*

b → v: Latin *fiber* → English *beaver*, *gubernare* → *govern*, *probare* → *prove*, *taberna* → *tavern*

c → ch: Old English *cealc* → English *chalk*, *cild* → *child*, *cin* → *chin*, *cirice* → *church*, *cyrn* → *churn*, *cyse* → *cheese*

c → g: Latin *acer* → English *eager*, *lacuna* → *lagoon*, *macer* → *meager*, *vinum+acre* → *vinegar*

c → h: Latin *canis* → English *hound*, *capere* → *harvest*, *centa*

→ *hundred*, *cervus* → *hart*, *collis* → *hill*, *cordis* → *heart*, *cornu* → *horn*

c → k: Old English *broc* → English *brook*, *cnoll* → *knoll*, *cyng* → *king*, *cynn* → *kin*

cg → dg: Old English *brycg* → English *bridge*, *ecg* → *edge*, *hrycg* → *ridge*

cw → qu: Old English *acwencan* → English *quench*, *cweccan* → *quake*, *cwen* → *queen*

d → t: Latin *cordis* → English *heart*, *decem* → *ten*, *dentis* → *tooth*, *domare* → *tame*, *duo* → *two*, *drys* → *tree*, *edere* → *eat*; Sanskrit *udra* → English *otter*

f → b: Latin *fagus* → English *beech*, *fero* → *bear* (as a verb), *fiber* → *beaver*, *frater* → *brother*

f → d: Latin *facere* → English *do*, *fingere* → *dough*, *foris* → *door*

f → v: Old English *beofor* → English *beaver*, *graf* → *grove*, *heofon* → *heaven*, *lufu* → *love*

g → k/ch: Latin *ager* → English *acre*, *gela* → *cold*, *gena* → *chin*, *genu* → *knee*, *genus* → *kin*, *(g)noscere* → *know*, *granum* → *corn*

g → y: Old Danish *garth* → English *yard*; Old Icelandic *garn* → English *yarn*, *gella* → *yell*, *girna* → *yearn*; Old English *ger* → English *year*, *gist* → *yeast*

h → g: Latin *hortus* → English *garden*, *hostis* → *guest*

h → gh: Old English *genoh* → English *enough*, *liht* → *light*, *niht* → *night*; Middle English *mihte* → English *might*

hw → wh: Old English *hwael* → English *whale*, *hwaer* → *where*, *hwaete* → *wheat*, *hwelp* → *whelp*, *hwit* → *white*, *hwy* → *why* h → Ø: Old English _hleapan_ → English _leap_, _hlot_ → _lot_, _hnutu_ → _nut_, _hrathor_ → _rather_, _hring_ → _ring_

> Note: _h_ has been dropped and added many different times, resulting in awkward forms like _habit_ or _herb_, where it is not entirely clear why the _h_ is present or whether it should be pronounced. Historical confusion over the use (and pronunciation) of _h_ is preserved in pairs of common names like _Art/Arthur_, _Dot/Dorothy_, _Kate/Katherine_, _Tom/Thomas_, _Tony/Anthony_.

i → y: Old English _bi_ → English _by_, _giet_ → _yet_, _iw_ → _yew_

p → f: Latin _pater_ → English _father_, _penna_ → _feather_, _pes_ → _foot_, _piscis_ → _fish_

p → v: Latin _cooperire_ → English _cover_, _paupertas_ → _poverty_, _praepositus_ → _provost_, _rapere_ → _ravish_, _recipere_ → _receive_, _riparius_ → _river_, _sapor_ → _savor_, _separare_ → _sever_

sc → sh: Old English _fisc_ → English _fish_, _sceap_ → _sheep_, _scip_ → _ship_, _scir_ → _shire_, _scofl_ → _shovel_, _sculdor_ → _shoulder_

t → th: Latin _tres_ → English _three_, _tenuis_ → _thin_, _tonare_ → _thunder_, _tumere_ → _thumb_

t → Ø: Latin _decretum_ → English _decree_, _frater_ → _friar_, _maritare_ → _marry_, _nativus_ → _naïve_, _rotundus_ → _round_, _vitabilis_ → _viable_, _votum_ → _vow_

u → o: Latin _buxus_ → English _box_, _cuprum_ → _copper_, _furca_ → _fork_; Old English _cume_ → English _come_, _lufu_ → _love_, _sunu_ → _son_, _wulf_ → _wolf_

u → ou: Old English _cu_ → English _cow_, _ful_ → _foul_, _hus_ → _house_, _mus_ → _mouse_, _ut_ → _out_

v → w: Latin _vallus_ → English _wall_, _vinum_ → _wine_

y → i: Old English _brycg_ → English _bridge_, _cyng_ → _king_, _cynn_ → _kin_ y → u: Old English *cyrn* → English *churn*

§

BUILDING WITH SYLLABLES

WHEN YOU START experimenting with ways of taking words apart and putting pieces together in new combinations, it will help if you understand the underlying structure of syllables, because syllabic units and the boundaries between syllabic units are the basic building blocks of words. Syllables are understood to be the natural sound units that occur in words; most words contain more than one syllable, but quite a few words consist of a single syllable.

In all cases, syllables can have three possible components. The *onset* is an initial consonant sound that opens the syllable, as in the *t* of *top*. The remaining letters of a syllable are called the *rime* because this is the portion of the syllable that can rhyme with other syllables; for example, *-op* is the rime of the syllables *top, pop, mop, sop*. Rimes are further subdivided into *nucleus*, which is the central portion of the syllable and usually consists of one or more vowels (e.g., the *-o-* in *-op*), and *coda*, which closes the syllable with one or more consonant sounds (e.g., the *-p* in *-op*).

Onsets and codas are optional, but every syllable contains a nucleus and in a few cases consists solely of a nucleus, as in *eye*. In general, however, nearly all syllables have both an onset and a nucleus, as in *ba-na-na* (a word where the syllable breaks naturally fall to create expected onset-nucleus combinations). In fact, if you look for consonants in words, you can often tell where syllabic breaks should occur.

An understanding of this basic structure might be helpful because when you place word elements in new combinations, or if you build new words, you are bound to produce unfamiliar sequences of letters, and some sequences of letters might need to be altered if they do not already suggest properly formed syllables. For instance, if you were the first person to add the suffix *-ation* to the word *magnify* you would be looking at the awkward combination *magnifyation*, which would need to be massaged into a more sensible form like *magnification* by inserting a *c* to create the sequence of strong syllables: *mag-ni-fi-ca-tion*. Your word *magnifyation* would never work, but by paying attention to syllables and simply adding a strong *c* at the right location, you can create a word that might last hundreds of years.

❧

As all languages age, their words simplify and monosyllables come to predominate over the long musical words of earlier times.

❧

CREATING ON AN OFFBEAT

IF YOU EXPERIMENT with changing the letters or sounds of words, keep in mind that it will be far easier to make changes in unaccented syllables. This is true because the accented "root syllable" of a word bears most of that word's etymological meaning and linguistic weight. And because root syllables carry so much of a word's weight, it means that the other syllables in a word can usually be dropped, altered, or diminished with minimal effect on the word.

It is easy to see that the accented syllables in words like _riv_-er and _moun_-tain carry the primary etymological meaning of these words. This gives you some freedom to change the other syllables and create novel words like _riva/rivor/rivis_ or _mountein/mountimo/mountung_ that still express the same root meanings—but in new ways.

❧

_Speak of what it feels like to be alive at this
moment of human (un)consciousness._

_Speak of "being conscious," alive to present, alive to responsibility,
not afraid to care, willing to feel the world alive._

❧

PRODUCTIVITY

AS DEFINED BY LINGUISTS, _productivity_ refers to any process that leads to the production of new forms (mainly new words). Productivity is an organizing principle highlighting the ways that some processes produce copious crops of new words, while other processes fade into obscurity. This is a valuable concept because it circles back to the important idea that languages exist only in communities, and only in communities can new language processes take root and blossom. So if your goal is to make sincere and positive contributions to your language, then you have to keep your community in mind, because spurious, ill-founded contributions will have little chance of lingering if they are not productive.

An example of productivity would be the suffix *-er*, which has a vibrant, almost limitless capacity to be added to words to create new words that name occupations (e.g., *farmer, lawyer, logger*) or objects that carry out actions (e.g., *computer, printer, typewriter*). Language elements like *-er* become productive because they survive their original impulse and continue to awaken language-generating energy over time. A process is therefore fruitful if it sparks the imagination of its community of users and comes to serve a vital purpose.

However, even the most fruitful processes may have periods of productivity and nonproductivity. Such is the case with *-ment*, a suffix that was highly productive in the late 1500s, when it was used to create over seven hundred nouns of action or condition (e.g., *agreement, implement, settlement*), but which has not been active in the formation of new words for several hundred years.

At the other end of the scale are word-making processes that feel awkward or fail to take root from the very onset. Some processes simply do not awaken the imagination of a community or do not find their way into a growing body of words. An example in English might be any attempt to create new words with doubled suffixes. Thus, English speakers instinctively reject words like *foolishish* or *uselessless* as unproductive, and even if one example of a word like this were to survive, it would not lead to the production of other similar forms.

There do not seem to be any hard-and-fast rules governing whether a process might be productive or not. Partly it depends on who uses a new word or process for the first time, or whether it is used in the telling of a popular story (famous or influential people, widely read stories, and events that stand out in the public consciousness all have a way of making unfamiliar new words or processes acceptable). For instance, the word *hobbit* is forever seared in the popular imagination due to the success of J. R. R. Tolkien's *Lord of the Rings* trilogy (though *hobbit* has not been productive in the formation of other words). Or consider the two related suffixes *-tion* and *-sion*, which Chaucer used productively in the formation of 199 unique words in *The Canterbury Tales* (he was not necessarily the first writer to use each of these words, but he was the first to use them so extensively that they entered popular usage).

But new word-making processes cannot simply rely on the boost of an influential person or story; they must carry their own weight by being at least somewhat attentive to the traditional sounds and shapes of their language. For instance, strings of consonants tend to feel awkward in English, so any process that results in letter combinations like *-rlsf-*, as in the made-up word *churlsful*, would probably never be productive. On the other hand, there is no reason why the Old English suffix *-cund* could not be made productive again, since it has a sound and shape that could be combined with many Modern English words (e.g., *seacund* 'sea-like,' or *stonecund* 'stone-like').

Productivity does not focus on individual words that have become popular or useful; it focuses instead on processes that lead to the formation of large groups of words. With this in mind it is worth collecting and keeping your eyes open for potentially productive word-forming processes. Old, inactive processes, such as overlooked and forgotten suffixes, are one place to start (though these processes may have been abandoned because they were replaced by newer, more productive processes or they have already exhausted the entire list of proper combinations). Alternatively, you could invent new processes, such as new suffixes or new ways of marking parts of speech, or you could adapt processes from other languages that have not been used in English before (which is where Chaucer derived much of his legendary word-making prowess). There are many untested processes lurking in largely forgotten languages like Old Norse, Old French, and Old English; look around and see if any might help you in your writing.

§.

Use old language rules that are valid because tested, and play—
bring language to life.

§.

NEW WORD FORMATION

IT WILL ALWAYS be helpful if you approach the creation of new words as a thoughtful and well-intentioned undertaking. After all, you are building something of significant and potentially lasting value for your culture, so this act should not be random or careless.

Linguists formally identify two conditions under which new words can be formed: there has to be something for the word to denote (to signify or point to), and there has to be a need for the new word. Words persist only when they are taken up and used by larger communities of people, and people usually take up new words that fill previously unoccupied niches about which they want to speak.

In a way, it is fortunate for writers that we live in a largely nature-illiterate society because this leaves an immense variety of conditions, aspects, moods, relationships, and settings in the natural world that are available to be recognized and named. The path to a growing awareness of the natural world will be paved with inspiring new words, and in turn these new words will make it fun and exciting to look at the world with a fresh perspective.

The first condition posed by linguists—that there has to be something to denote—should be no problem for alert writers; you can start by considering the many aspects of the natural world waiting to be named. Keep in mind the classic story (whether or not it is true) that Eskimos have dozens of words to name the different types of what English speakers simply call "snow," because this story suggests that even the simplest of objects invites many new layers of words.

The second condition linguists highlight—that there has to be a need for a new word—is precisely the work expected of writers. You create a need for new words by telling good stories that speak of situations in which those words have a context.

Creating new words isn't so hard: just find the empty spaces of the world that are waiting to be named and fill them with life.

ૐ

Each of us has to save one fish, not because it saves the ocean, but because it matters to at least one fish.

In a time of discouragement and dismay at what is happening to the environment and to our ability to influence political processes, there is great power in finding creative tools that keep our spirits alive and hopeful.

ૐ

BECOMING ANIMAL

DAVID ABRAM proposes in his book *Becoming Animal* that we have lost touch with the most important relationship of all: the interweaving of our sensate bodies with an equally sensate cosmos. Tracing how words have become self-enclosed systems of symbolic communication, and how knowledge has become an abstracted realm of information relegated to the mind and mediated by "experts," Abram offers an alternate view that language is not simply a human possession and thoughts do not arise within the human skull. He suggests instead that language and thoughts arise from the creativity of our entire bodies as we respond to our environment. In fact, Abram suggests that *mind* does not reside within us, but that we reside within *mind*, and that everything around us participates equally in this mind because it is a "property of the earth itself."

In modern society we have created a very lonely existence for ourselves by separating our thoughts and language from the world, making them exclusively human properties, and then restricting them to the brains housed in our skulls. Words are now frozen on flat pages and screens and viewed as lifeless symbols rather than active participants in the world, while in oral cultures words signaled a spacious and active engagement between a social group and its landscape. Remember Abram's image of Tibetan monks taking woodblocks of carved prayers and stamping them on the surface of a flowing river over and over again as if actively and physically imprinting the woodblock prayers on the three-dimensional surface of the world.

This is language that is alive, and Abram might suggest that the world is stamping its language on us in the same way. Pay attention to the ways your body responds to the world; listen for the language of the animals, of trees, rocks, and clouds. We live in a world vibrant with life, energy, language, and mind; listen closely and you will discover that all of your intelligent animal body is in constant communication with this alive and beautiful world.

❧

Find the strength to recall the Muses from their banishment.

Search hard for values, ideals, and aesthetic sensibilities
that are lacking in our modern era: ideals of responsibility,
ethical relationship to the nonhuman world, emotional
content, and respect for generations beyond our own
(both forward and backward):
THESE ARE THE IDEALS THAT NEED LANGUAGE ...
this is the task, the slow putting together of
discovered values and discovered language.

❧

LOCAL LANGUAGE

I BELIEVE THAT the greatest role of language is to give each community of people a voice for speaking of their unique place in the cosmic sweep of the universe. It could be said that languages are conversations between peoples and their known landscapes and that the identity of a people begins and ends with the land they inhabit.

Sadly, it might also be said that languages begin to die when

240

people stop paying attention to the land that is their home. Without the presence of an "other" found in the land, language becomes self-referential and fades into solipsism. Remember to always hold the land in your language-making exercises and do not drift off into the mirrored cleverness of your own thoughts.

§

Let us serve the Muses while the meadows are still untouched.
—modified from Choerilus, fifth-century BC poet

§

WISDOM

WISDOM HAS BEEN practiced in many ways over the course of human history, but in his book *Wisdom Sits in Places* Keith Basso describes an approach followed by the Western Apache of east-central Arizona that I particularly like.

Basso says that wisdom arises from three mental conditions. First you must cultivate "smoothness of mind" by clearing away the obstructions and clutter that can cloud your insights like dirt on a window. Then you must develop "resilience of mind" in the same way that a tightly woven basket holds its shape yet is flexible in the face of external forces. And finally you must secure "steadiness of mind" so that you can hold firm against internal deviations in the same way that a post driven into the ground holds its place.

Basso cautions that the path leading to wisdom is exhausting and most people give up at some point, while only a few persevere and continue questioning the implications of life's choices and actions at deeper and deeper levels.

Ultimately it probably does not matter how you approach wisdom, just that you do approach wisdom and a carefully considered moral life in some way. This is a vital human act, yet most of us become sidetracked in our busy, complex lives. As Basso writes, "The human mind is a vulnerable space, and protecting it against obstacles that threaten incisive thinking is a formidable task."

Each of us, therefore, has to vigilantly guard and nurture the development of our minds, and we must all do the hard work of finding our path and turning away from the distractions that harm our capacity to grow and serve. By necessity, this means filtering out many of the distracting products and gimmicks of modern society in favor of an older and deeper wisdom. This is why we, like the Western Apache, should turn to the land, to the natural world, and to old stories for guidance.

If new words arise from this place of wisdom, then this will be a blessing, part of the rhythmic heartbeat of language that connects the past to the future and keeps us all alive.

ও

Taking out the compost, I leave a trail in the wild grasses.

ও